Career Guide

How to Become a Pathfinder for Lifetime Success

(How to Make Your Work Life More Fulfilling and Meaningful)

Nicole Oakes

Published By **Andrew Zen**

Nicole Oakes

All Rights Reserved

Career Guide: How to Become a Pathfinder for Lifetime Success (How to Make Your Work Life More Fulfilling and Meaningful)

ISBN 978-1-77485-589-8

No part of this guidebook shall be reproduced in any form without permission in writing from the publisher except in the case of brief quotations embodied in critical articles or reviews.

Legal & Disclaimer

The information contained in this ebook is not designed to replace or take the place of any form of medicine or professional medical advice. The information in this ebook has been provided for educational & entertainment purposes only.

The information contained in this book has been compiled from sources deemed reliable, and it is accurate to the best of the Author's knowledge; however, the Author cannot guarantee its accuracy and validity and cannot be held liable for any errors or omissions. Changes are periodically made to this book. You must consult your doctor or get professional medical advice before using any of the suggested remedies, techniques, or information in this book.

Upon using the information contained in this book, you agree to hold harmless the Author from and against any damages, costs, and expenses, including any legal fees potentially resulting from the application of any of the information provided by this guide. This disclaimer applies to any damages or injury caused by the use and application, whether directly or indirectly, of any advice or information presented, whether for breach of contract, tort, negligence, personal injury, criminal intent, or under any other cause of action.

You agree to accept all risks of using the information presented inside this book. You need to consult a professional medical practitioner in order to ensure you are both able and healthy enough to participate in this program.

Table of contents

Introduction _____ *1*

Chapter 1: Are You A Bitch Or A Beast? _____ *2*

Chapter 2: Can You Be Able To Get Out Of Cool Zones? _____ *5*

Chapter 3: How Transform Your Life Around ___ *10*

Chapter 4: Start With Small Things _____ *16*

Chapter 5: Have You Uncovered Your Purpose In Life? _____ *20*

Chapter 6: 11 Rich Habits That You Must Know *27*

Chapter 7: You Do Not Stop When You're Tired, But You Stop When You're Done _____ *32*

Chapter 8: Becoming A Scam Taker _____ *37*

Chapter 9: Creating A Planning _____ *43*

Chapter 10: Start Going On The Right Track ___ *87*

Chapter 11: Managing The Performance Appraisal _____ *135*

Conclusion _____ *179*

INTRODUCTION

An old Wiseman once stated "Someone once advised me not to eat more than I'm able to chew. I replied that I'd rather choke on the greatness instead of nibbling on dullness."

If you look around and observe the world around you, you'll realize that the majority of people including us, live average or less than ideal lives. We are constantly putting off the things we really wish for and long to achieve, only to end up getting aged and incapable of achieving our dreams.

A lifetime of time has been wasted in the same way, but no one seems to realize the reason why they're constantly doing wrong. If you're in the same rut now is the time to get out. Today you'll discover the ways you can break free of the chain that are tying you in this situation and not settle for an average performance. You will finally fly higher than you ever have previously and be a glowing stars in the sky. This is the day to say no to the average.

CHAPTER 1: ARE YOU A BITCH OR A BEAST?

Today, most people are living normal lives. They are accustomed to a schedule for their week that seldom alters. This routine has them nowhere. They're not growing as human beings, nor are they developing spiritually or mentally. They're just like machines that are programmed to perform the same routine day after day. They are under the assumption that the routine they're living is the right one for them since that's what other people doing too. But what a lot of people aren't aware of is that they possess the ability to change their lives. Human beings are able to use them to create transformations in their lives. One thing they don't always know or aren't aware of is how to bring the change.

Are you always annoyed and bored? If the answer is Yes, there could be various reasons why you feel this way. It's crucial to recognize that when you feel depressed and angry it's often because you're living an unsatisfactory life aligned with your dreams and ideals. This kind of frustration, boredom and irritation is a sign and a signal to you that you must change something in your life.

If you're wondering how you can make these changes happen within your own life, today we'll provide you with a few strategies to turn your life around in the process of moving forward.

What you must do get moving forward is examine where you stand. Do you have a routine life that's heading nowhere? Do you feel stuck in the same routine that is never able to be changing or live the kind of life where every day is different and there is something to be looking towards? Are you stuck as the little tinkerer who is always being directed by others, or are you the one who has total and total authority over all your activities? Once you know your position and where you are, it is time to make the next move. Keep in mind that you have the power within you to effect the necessary and significant transformation within your own life. There is no reason to remain trapped in the same routine. It's time to quit living the normal and boring life and begin living an amazing and satisfying life. Don't be being one of those people who die with regrets. Instead, be part of the people who lead an exciting, joyful and thrilling life.

Making changes to your life doesn't require you to abandon the old routine and obligations. It's just that you achieve a healthy equilibrium between both in order to lead a life that's better than the average. It's not your destiny to do the job, pay your bills and then retire, without having lived. You were created to change the world, however you are small or large, you were made to live an exciting and exciting life and you were destined to fulfill your goals Don't let anything stop you and hinder you from reaching the heights you were designed to reach.

Chapter 2: Can You Be Able To Get Out Of Cool Zones?

Have you heard the phrase, "Life begins at the edge of your comfortable area."? Though many of us fail to comprehend this notion of breaking free from our comfortable zones If you really want to live a fulfilled and higher-than-average life first thing you have to get out of your comfortable zone. We must first understand the concept of what your "comfort zone" signifies. The term "comfort zone" refers to the psychological state in which you are at ease, stress free and completely in control of your life. It's a state of having a state where your fears are minimized and you are always able to access to a variety of essentials and necessities like food and shelter, clothing, and other essential things.

If you're the type of person with a stable job, a fixed sources of earnings, a steady life, routines that repeat and all-around the security and stability you desire You are in your comfortable zone. While this safe and secure life style may help reduce anxiety and stress however, it forces you to live a lifestyle which is normal. It's not necessarily an ideal or bad choice to be in your comfortable area, but it will not ever allow you to grow as a person. You'll always be bound by invisible chains that block any form of mental or spiritual development.

Let's take a look at why people are scared to step outside of his familiar zone. Imagine living a lifestyle in which you don't have a stable and secure job, and your income source fluctuates, imagine every day differing from the last and you never having a security and assured throughout your day. You're probably thinking an uncertain and unpredictable life would just increase your anxiety and stress, keeping you anxious and uneasy. It's the very anxiety of these fears that stops the majority of people from stepping out of their comfortable areas. What most people do not realize is that their comfortable zone is only an illusion. It's a lie because there is nothing that can be assured. Who knows what tomorrow will bring? There is a chance that you will get lucky or even get unexpectedly struck by a car. The world is not full of guarantee and each person's destiny is, in the end, is the same: death. Yet, people will keep to their comfort zones because it gives them with a sense of safety even if the feeling of security and stability is only an illusion.

Do you feel that fear of failure stop you from taking on something that you've always envisioned? Are you able to think of some great business concepts in your mind but are hesitant to pursue the idea because you're afraid to take the risk and more hesitant to fail? The fear of failing will hinder you from taking on the most innovative ideas. You will just stay safe and live your normal life. Think about the billionaires, the ever changing leaders and entrepreneurs Are you wondering what they have done differently that puts them above others? It's because they are risk-averse and take risks, but the most important thing is that they break out of their familiar areas. This doesn't mean they're not as scared of failure like you, but their fear of failing is stronger than their fear of failing and eventually leads to them becoming successful leaders and entrepreneurs.

"The key to success is to go down seven times and climb back up eight times." Global leaders businessmen, billionaires, entrepreneurs and other famous personalities have plenty of setbacks however, those mistakes are just the first steps to success. A determination and not-giving-up attitude is what distinguishes individuals who are successful from the average ones. In order to stand out from the crowd it is not necessary to be afraid of failure Instead, you should be afraid of not trying.

If you're looking for ways to step out of your comfortable zone, here's some ideas you can do. A very efficient and simple ways to step from your routine is taking a different approach every day. It doesn't have to be a huge undertaking or even simple like taking a different way to work, not drinking the alcohol for a few days or having ice cream for breakfast, or other things. It will assist in reestablishing your understanding of reality. Recalibrating your perception of reality will help in breaking away from the routine of life and allowing into account different perspectives.

Another method of getting from your routine is taking the time to consider your options. This is crucial for those who lead hectic life and don't get the opportunity to slow down and breathe. It can assist you in breaking from that gruelling routine and also your familiar zone. Take your time and take a deep breath and think, analyze the information, then decide to act. In the event you're the type of person who spends long periods of time making decisions, you must do the opposite to move out of your comfortable zone. Make an instant and unintentional decision. Making a quick , impulsive choice will help you to trusting in your judgment and intuition and will aid in breaking out of your comfortable zone.

It is also natural that breaking out your comfort zone might appear like a daunting job to you. It isn't necessary to be nervous or anxious about getting out of your comfort zone. If you're worried and anxious about leaving your comfortable zone consider doing small steps to take the necessary steps. It's not necessary to right into a leap. Begin slowly and gradually by taking each step one at a gradual pace and you'll discover it easier to get out of the routine and get comfortable. Therefore, stop worrying about the possibility of be a failure and instead, shift your attention to doing something that you've previously been afraid to attempt before.

Chapter 3: How Transform Your Life Around

Are you ready to change you life upside down? Are you willing to live a life the majority of people imagine? If you really would like to bring great transformations in your life, the first question you have to consider is whether you're truly frustrated and dissatisfied by living a boring life. It is essential to reach the point in your life that you can't bear to endure another second in the exact same way. You must be so annoyed with your life for the fact that you are mediocre to the point where it could cause you to go insane if you had to face each day. When you reach this stage changing your life is simple.

If you've reached the tipping point in your life, you have to take a decisive choice about making changes within your own life. Making a decision on your own isn't enough. You have to make sincere and constant efforts to see it through. It is essential to take a firm commitment to yourself if desire to change things around. If you believe that you are physically and mentally ready to make the first step towards an even more satisfying and satisfying life, then you'll begin making your life better than before.

The next step to turn your life around making a decision to implement certain changes in your daily routine. Here are some tips you can use to begin making changes. It is a good idea to read every day. is extremely beneficial in transforming your life. Although it might appear as, reading is a type of relaxation that can calm your mind. Apart from the wonderful relaxing effects of reading, it also stimulates your brain and keeps it alert and focused. Reading is a way to escape the squalor of your daily life and into a realm of endless possibilities and excitement. So reading on a regular basis is highly suggested. Some people aren't fans of reading however, therefore, look into other options such as audiobooks but don't forget to take advantage of the information that can change your life. world offers.

Another great way to turn things around in your own life would be recording your dreams aspirations, goals and aspirations. In the hustle and bustle of everyday life we can forget about what we're thinking about; and we also tend to lose our thoughts and objectives. Write down your goals to assist in staying on track and getting them accomplished faster.

The relationships we have with others play an important aspect of our lives. If you're not in the right type of relationship and you want to change your life, it isn't easy. Therefore, take control of your life by eliminating the relationships that cause destruction and destruction within your life. Be aware that you must surround yourself with those who inspire you and not make you feel stressed out. Remove all the people from your life that are restricting or hindering your growth development. Although this will be very difficult but it is the best way to take it in order to ensure the improvement of your life.

Exercise and healthy eating can have a profound impact on your life. If you're feeling physically and mentally healthy and happy, it will bring about positive things to happen in your life. Make sure you eat healthy and consume healthy and nutritious foods , and also do a daily exercise regular basis. You will be amazed at the changes you see to your lifestyle.

The idea of saving some money to cover a rainy day is also highly advised. Even if you are struggling to pay the bills however, even small savings over a month is highly suggested. Savings regularly will help you in the future , or if ever you find yourself experiencing any sort of difficulty.

The idea of starting your own business may seem like a flimsy idea to you, however, working for someone else is very difficult and stressful. The work you do may not be appreciated or you may not be satisfied with your professional profile and other things like that. When you're launching your own business doesn't mean you should quit your job. It is possible to run your business from your spare time. It doesn't have to be an expensive and lengthy undertaking. Your business could just be selling something you've made yourself. For example, if you're skilled at crocheting, you can sell handbags and crochet sweaters while you are at it If you're an accomplished artist, you could sell the work you create in your spare time, and the list goes on. Being a business owner is an exhilarating and thrilling experience and could be a great way of changing your life.

Get off the stupid box. The constant viewing of television can make you feel numb and also a complete unnecessary waste of time. Instead of spending all day at a time watching television instead, do something productive and worthwhile. Find a passion or do things that make you think.

Do you have something that you're interested in? Every person is enthusiastic about something. This could include painting, singing, writing or something else. It is time to you can indulge in your passion again. Engaging in something you truly enjoy can be a source of joy and result in major changes to your lifestyle. If you are unhappy at work or are engaged in activities you do not like, you're going to feel stressed and annoyed constantly. If you really want to transform your life, concentrate on what you're truly interested in.

A vacation can assist you in getting get back on track and aid in making changes within your own life. Every now and again, we need to put aside, take a break from our daily routine, relax and visit a new place to gain an objective view of our lives. Therefore, get away even for a brief trip and it can help get your mind off of the sand and help you know what you'd like to make within your routine and in your daily life.

If you truly want to change your life make small improvements however, you must START! Implement these strategies within your everyday life. Start small if you don't have the circumstances to make a big deal of it. Remember that you shouldn't do the same thing over and over again and expect different outcomes. Go out and explore all the possibilities that the universe offers.

Chapter 4: Start With Small Things

What you'll need to do is to inject a lot of love to your life. What can you do to achieve this? In order to bring happiness into your life, you must be a part of the community and spread love. It is possible to do this through simple actions like giving three people each day with genuine praise. You could also visit to help those in need and get involved in the welfare of animals and even volunteer in elderly care homes. If you're truly and completely sharing with love and affection, you're never going to be unhappy or bored.

Another method that is extremely effective in helping you break out of the cycle is being in the natural world. It has been proven scientifically fact that people who spend some time in the outdoors every day, are less likely to be anxious and depressed. Many people are stuck with their lives. Their routines consist of an 8-to-5 work schedule and returning home during rush hour, spending time with their family and eating dinner before retiring to their bedrooms. Through this routine they have no time to breathe in breathing in fresh air or to exercise , and most importantly, they don't have time to themselves. If you spend an hour in the nature, or walking for a long time along the shore, in the woods, or in the park can be very beneficial to the mental and physical health of those who take it. In addition to mental and physical well-being Nature has a way of creating happiness, and can boost your immune system. A good dose of sunlight is vital to your overall health. The sun's rays boost the Vitamin D levels within the body, and has been shown to lower the risk of developing fatal diseases such as cancer. Therefore, if you truly want to break free of the dreadful routine, go outside every day and refresh your body and mind.

It may sound odd, but an effective method of breaking out of your routine and routine is to speak the truth. When you next find yourself at a conference or meeting do not be afraid to express your opinion and confidently present your viewpoint. If you notice that your team is experiencing tension, don't be afraid to voice your opinion. Being honest has the unique ability of freeing you. It can bring about a degree of enthusiasm and excitement within your daily life. In its own unique way, telling the truth will gently break you out of your routine.

Do you have any memories of the hobbies you enjoyed as a kid? Paint, gardening, sports music, writing, as well as other enjoyable and creative activities, try to find time in the day to enjoy them again. Engaging in your passions can help you lose your identity as well as space and time. This this will help you get in tune with the natural rhythm of your life. This can enable you to break free from the annoying routine you've been stuck in.

Another way to break out of the rut is making use of your own natural talents and abilities. If, for instance, you're a gifted musician or motivational speaker however, your position is accounting. You have to take the time to incorporate motivational speaking as well as singing in your daily routine. It is possible to set some time during the daytime to practice singing or go for a sing-along every once in a while to a bar that has karaoke. As a motivational speaker you can deliver motivational talks to children students, and other people who could really benefit from the motivational power to make progress and take important choices in their lives. Maintaining your natural talent and growing is an excellent method to transform your life positively.

CHAPTER 5: HAVE YOU UNCOVERED YOUR PURPOSE IN LIFE?

"The reason for living is to live with purpose"- Robert Byrne

Finding a reason in your life is vitally important. You shouldn't be doing life with the same old routine without a sense of reason, as you'll eventually be unhappy. If you live your life with no purpose at the time you're old and look back on your younger years, you'll be able to look back and regret the boring and meaningless life you lived. Let us first discover what the purpose of life really is.

When we talk about"purpose", we're not talking about your routine chores, daily tasks and responsibilities. What we're referring to is the main motive that drives your existence.

Do you find yourself going about your life with a sense of devoidness or sense that there is something missing from your life? This feeling could happen to you especially in an age in which a lot of emotional changes are happening. The feeling of being empty is especially intense when you realize that you're not immortal. If an unplanned event is a surprise on a Tuesday morning, and provides you with the chance to see your death, you begin to think about and doubt your real purpose and more profound meaning behind your existence.

For centuries , philosophers have been focusing on the significance of living. Although this is a controversial and philosophical subject but it has a profound significance. When a person is aware of and comprehends the reason for his existence, it provides him with the motivation to continue to live his life with excitement looking towards. If you've not yet identified your life's purpose now is the time to spend some time to discover it. Let's discuss how you can discover the purpose of your life.

The process of determining your goal is often an uphill endeavor and could require a lot self-questioning and reflection. You must know some very fundamental things concerning yourself, before you determine what your purpose in life. It is important to take your time alone and contemplate certain questions. You must look within yourself, be in the present and not rely on the external circumstances and events. When you've figured out the answers to some crucial questions, the purpose of your life will likely be revealed before you. Let's discuss a few issues you should think on.

Use a pencil and paper, lie in a comfortable position with your mobile turned off, stay clear of an unattractive environment and start. If you can, when you answer these types of questions, attempt to be as quick as you can and also be sincere. There's no need to prove anything here , and the answers are yours only, so don't lie about the way you feel. Try to finish your answers in less than 60 seconds. Start with the first thing that pops up in your mind when you ask yourself and you don't have to take time to come up with the answer. The answers must be a natural instinctual response. Do not think about it, grab your pen and paper and get it done now!

Here's the first question you should think about.

1. What brings you joy?

It could be any thing. This could include your friends, family activities, work, or any other event. If you are asked the question, immediately note down your responses. It's one of the things that comes to your mind. The next thing you have to consider is what you loved doing back in the day, and what do you are currently enjoying. Note down the responses for both scenarios and then compare the two.

Note down what is unchanged in the past and what has changed.

2. What is it that gives you a sense of the purpose of your life?

The next question to consider is those hobbies or activities you love so much that you completely lose feeling of time, space and yourself while engaging with these activities. It could be anything like singing, painting and other creative arts such as programming, gardening, and a myriad of others. These activities are so thrilling and relaxing for you that there is nothing else that really matters when you're immersed in these activities. Write down the very first response you get whenever you ask yourself questions about the things you love to do.

3. What makes you feel great?

Ask yourself what it is that makes you feel good and confident about yourself. It could be anything, it could depend on your abilities to assist others, your ability to sing, or everything else. After this you will need to ask yourself which people truly inspire and inspire you. This could include your close family members and acquaintances, strangers and authors world leaders, or nearly any other person. These are the people you would like to be like as well as your role as models. Write down names that appear in your mind Don't take enough time to think about them.

4. Which are some of your most natural talents?

The next thing you'll have to ask is: What is your natural gift you were born with. Something you're really proficient in and confident in doing without hesitation. Some people's natural talents include singing, art or math, others are blessed with talents such as healing, or a keen sense of and other such. You can find your gifts by asking what assistance people typically need from you. If, for instance they are seeking advice and to discuss their problems it could be your goal to become a healer or psychologist. If they come to you to repair their plants that are dying Your purpose in life could be tied to gardening, giving your time to environmental causes and the list goes on.

5. What could you do to add worth for the rest of humanity?

Ask yourself, if you were given the chance to instruct something that you're proficient at, what would be. Note down the first thought that pops into your head. You can then follow this with a question about what is in your life you'd be regretful of not doing or being. Ask yourself what values you possess within you that you consider to be unique. These can include the qualities of leadership, motivation, creativity and honesty. They could also be integrity, integrity, honesty or other positive qualities.

6. What is your message to the world?

The next thing you should be focusing on is to ask yourself about specific difficulties and rough patches in your life that you had to overcome in the past, and what you did to overcome the challenges. The next one you should be asking yourself is what are the things that you truly believe in and have an affinity for and if you could send an important message across the globe, what would convey and what type of message you would convey.

After you've written down your skills and talents, capabilities and values, as well as things you are passionate about, ask yourself how you can make use of these assets to influence the world in a positive manner. After you've jotted down the responses to the questions above Create a complete list of specific action words. They could be motivational speech, intuition, leadership and many more. The words that people use to describe their actions might differ depending on the answers they provide. Then, ask yourself how you can assist some particular person or animal or an organization by using your actions words. Find out who can get the most benefit from your skills and talents. If you can answer to these questions, you'll get an instant understanding of your purpose in life. When you've done this all you have to do is be a believer in yourself and take part in your part to make the world one that is better.

Chapter 6: 11 Rich Habits That You Must Know

Achieving a better life than the norm means increasing your overall prosperity and wealth. If you want to lead a happy and wealthy life, it is essential to implement certain changes in your everyday life. Did you ever think to you that those who are wealthy adhere to certain routines that less fortunate and the average person are often ignorant of. Now, you do not have to live in the shadows. We'll show you about the changes that you should implement into your everyday life if you are looking to get away from the crowd and experience the success you deserve. Here's the checklist:

Reading: Reading is the ability to stimulate the mind, and keeps readers sharp and engaged. Reading is a great way to increase understanding and also plays an important part in self-improvement. The wealthy take time in their schedules to read, even when it's only for only a few minutes. When we say read it doesn't mean you must read romance novels or comics novels. Instead it is essential to discover books that are stimulating for your mind. Study self-improvisation books and other books that aid in your understanding of the human condition as well as important statistics, culture as well as other essential aspects of our lives.

Ask Questions about Your Faith If you really want to improve as a human being , and possibly break free from the miserable life you're stuck in, it is time to start challenging your beliefs and challenging your assumptions. If you remain adamant about the same views, you'll end up stuck in a routine which is based on your convictions. The wealthy are open in their mind, they challenge their beliefs, they attempt to think outside of the box, and they are a part of people who challenge them and allow them to think in a different way. The rich have a wide mind that's not tied to one set of values.

Future-oriented planning is essential if you want to achieve success then you must plan things that will prove to benefit you in the near future. It is essential to be able to see for what the future holds. You must be ready to face any obstacles that could occur within the next few years. Therefore, you should anticipate the future, it's an activity that the wealthy are known to indulge in.

Exercise: Don't think you don't have time. You have the exact amount of time per working day Albert Einstein had. It doesn't matter if must get at a certain time or fall asleep two hours later, you can find time during the day to workout. If you want to succeed then you must be able to enjoy success while maintaining good health. Regular exercise helps maintain good physical as well as mental health. The most successful people always find their time to work out and if you would like to live the same lifestyle as them, then you must make time in your schedule to work out.

Concentrate on the Important Decisions Human beings have to make a lot of decisions every day. These include crucial ones like life or business decisions , as well as minor ones such as how to dress or eating. What do the wealthy do in these situations? They are focused on making the most important issues. They invest all of their efforts to make decisions that are essential to their lives and their businesses, and don't pay attention to the minor things such as what to eat or what clothes to wear. If you'd like to live like the wealthy make sure you do everything to get rid of the mundane and concentrate on the important ones.

Keep a To-Do list It is a fact that the most successful and successful people have a regular to-do list. However, just keeping the list isn't enough. You need to adhere to it. If you have a specific number of tasks that you have to finish in a certain time frame ensure that you finish these tasks. Being lazy and slacking will keep you from achieving your goals.

Begin to Meet New People: This habit is especially recommended for people who aren't confident in being in public. Everyday interactions with new people will increase your confidence and help overcome the fear of speaking in front of large groups of people as well as in crowds.

Be a morning person When you wake up earlier, you'll take some time to relax. It is a good time to think, reflect and think about your day. People who are wealthy have the habit of getting up earlier and if you are looking to break out of the routine it is also advisable to begin waking up earlier.

Stop wasting your time using social media platforms and watching Television The social media platforms and TV boxes are temporary distractions that aid in numbing your mind and distracting from reality. Instead of trying escape from the harsh realities of everyday life, look for solutions that forever fix the issue. The richest people don't have to spend hours at a time in front of an dumb box or on social media platforms.

Be grateful: Another great way to be rich is being grateful. It is also important to be thankful for the small and big things that happen in your life. If someone is kind to you, that you are grateful to them, thank God for everything happening within your own life. If you're thankful then you'll be able to be able to attract more abundance into your life.

Living a simple life When it comes to material items, purchase only those you require and are necessary, but don't purchase things you don't want. A wise man once said "We purchase things that we don't require, with money we don't have to make people feel better about us." When you're looking to purchase expensive items to have fun then you're likely to be financially strained and lacking. We're not saying you should live your life like saints, but don't buy unnecessary items either.

If you're trying to enjoy the lifestyle that people who are wealthy live it's time to begin adopting these healthy ways of living into your day as soon as possible.

Chapter 7: You Do Not Stop When You're Tired,

But You Stop When You're Done

The process of breaking out of routine and making a leap from where you are isn't always simple. Humans are so content in our familiar surroundings that it's nearly impossible to leave them. When we finally make the choice to make modifications in our lives we are exhausted and frustrated trying to implement the changes. Henry Ford once said, "Obstacles are those terrifying things you notice when you turn your attention away from your target." The process of making changes to your life can be very demanding and if you come across difficulties on each path it is likely you'll be tempted to abandon the endeavor. To get rid of away that lackluster aspect of your life, you must to continue moving ahead until you achieve your destination.

Here are some suggestions to stay focused when you're feeling down and ready to quit:

Believe: To keep your motivation high, you must faith that what you're working towards will happen. There is no moment of doubt. It is essential to get up each morning, look yourself in the mirror , and affirm to your self, "I believe something wonderful will happen to me this day." You could make similar affirmations to manifest within your life. Whatever you're saying make sure you believe in it.

Don't Worry: Most of the things that we are worried about do not happen. Van Wilder once said, "Worrying is like rocking chair. It provides you with an activity to engage in, but it's not going to get you anywhere." So, you should stop worrying. Instead, give your absolute best and sincere efforts towards achieving your goal , and let the results be the responsibility of the universe. Remember that stressing can only make you feel less motivated.

Listen to and read about motivational stuff Listening to and reading positive and motivational content will help you stay positive and motivated. There are many motivational audiobooks, books as well as videos and songs that are available. If you're feeling low or unmotivated you can indulge in these motivational music and reading. They will help you stay motivated.

Be surrounded by positive people Positive people play a significant part in keeping you motivated. If you're in a group of negative and cynical individuals, you'll feel demotivated and depressed. Beware of people who have negative opinions. If you're ever caught in a crowd of people who are negative and there's no escape you, try to maintain an impartial perspective and refrain from taking part in the discussion.

Celebration: If you've completed even the tiniest of your tasks, you should take the opportunity to celebrate. If we say that you should"celebrate," we don't mean you should open an expensive bottle of expensive champagne. You could just purchase an amazing chocolate bar or the pleasure of a cup of coffee at your favorite coffee shop, and the list goes on. The reward you receive keeps you motivated to work toward your objective.

As we've established previously that making changes to your lifestyle can be difficult. There will times and feel that you're not able to continue, at times when you're tempted to quit but these are the times when you must remain determined and take a break from motivation and focus towards the final goal. We will now read some motivational speeches and inspirational quotes by prominent leaders and entrepreneurs that will inspire you to continue.

Steve Jobs "Your period of time is limited So don't waste your time by living the life of someone else. Don't be entangled by the dogma that is living by the outcomes of the thinking of others. Don't let other people's opinion drown out the sound of your inner voice. Most importantly, you must be brave enough to trust your gut and instincts. They already know the person you really would like to become. Everything else is secondary."

Marketing Slogans to promote Apple Inc.: Original

"Here's to the insane ones. The rebels. The misfits. The rebels. The troublemakers. Round pegs in square holes.

They see things in a different manner. They're not a fan of rules. They don't have a regard for the status established. They can be quoted and disagree with them. You can praise or denigrate them.

The only thing you can do is to ignore them. Because they are the ones who change things. They create. They think. They heal. They investigate. They make. They incite. They push humanity ahead.

They might be insane.

What else could you do but stare at a blank canvas and admire a work of art? You can also sit and listen to a song that has never been composed? Or stare at the red planet and discover a lab that is with wheels?

We design and manufacture tools that are suited to these types of people.

While many consider them mad ones, in reality, we view them as the genius. Because those who are insane enough to believe that they have the power to make a difference in the world will be the people who actually do."

When you feel down and feel like you're lacking the motivation to continue, take a look at these speeches. We are sure that you'll gain the strength to confront the challenges and over come the hurdles. Don't give up because you're tired, angry or tired, you can stop once you've achieved your objectives.

CHAPTER 8: BECOMING A SCAM TAKER

"There is no major achievement without the possibility of risk." Neil Armstrong. Neil Armstrong

If you want to make a change in your life, break free of the rut, and fuck the norm, you must to take chances. If you keep making walls, you'll end up stuck in your fortress. If you don't take risks it will be difficult to progress. You'll remain in your comfortable zone and you won't be able to discover the incredible opportunities life can offer.

Even though risk-taking can be terrifying and scary it's just something that you must take on to improve your skills. There is a chance that you will be hit, however there's the possibility that you will rise to new heights. If you are knocked down when you take a risk, all you have be reminded of is to get up, to attempt again, and attempt to take the plunge once more. In the end, after many knockdowns, will be enjoying the spotlight of your the success.

Let's talk about the risks that successful, happy and above average individuals take:

They're Not Afraid of being injured: The majority of us are scared of being hurt that we prefer to stay in our comfort zone, and try to avoid injury and take risks. The people who succeed make the leap without worry of being hurt. No whether they've suffered heartbreak It doesn't matter how many times they've been disappointed They won't cling for fear of repeating itself. They can move forward with confidence and are always willing to take on risks. So if you want to be different from the norm and become a better person, you must eliminate all doubts and be open to taking risks. One wise man declared, "Forget the risk and be willing to fall, if that's the outcome you're after, it's well worth it."

They're not afraid to be their authentic selves The Dr. Seuss was famous for his famous quote "Be yourself and speak what you think as those who don't mind do not matter and those who matter don't care." If you're constantly trying to please everyone in the world, you'll find yourself unhappy. You'll never be able to progress or develop as an individual. You will be a standard. Do not be afraid to speak out, voice your opinions and, most importantly, show your true self. There's no need to appear to be someone or someone you're not because you're afraid of making your real self known before the entire world. It isn't a matter of what other people say about you It's all about how you feel about yourself and how content you are. If someone doesn't like you as you are, that's their issue and not yours. Be yourself make a statement and take action to make yourself happy since life's too brief to be average.

It's OK to Miss Out on Certain Things We'll be honest, you're not able to have everything. If you purchase a brand new car, there'll likely be an update coming out of it soon. You must learn to appreciate the things you already have. If you are constantly looking for the next thing that's better it is not just that you get rid of the things you have, but you'll also never be satisfied with your life. It's not a game, and you don't need to chase after the next thing. Take advantage of the things you have, and put aside things you take as a given.

Don't Expect Anything in Exchange: If you're willing to do selfish things for others in the hope of receiving something in return, you're not going to ever break the average. The act of selflessness makes individuals feel happy and successful. Do not be afraid to take risks and assist those in need, smile at strangers, cheer up your family and friends, lift people up, and get involved with animal welfare. The most effective way to attain satisfaction is by making people smile.

Be Prepared to Take Full Responsibility for Your Own Happiness: You can't rely on anyone else to make you feel happy. Happiness is something that comes from within. It is essential to take the effort to become satisfied. It is not possible to blame others for the problems which are happening in your life. It is time to accept the risk of taking control of your happiness. If you begin playing the blame game , it implies that you're not taking on the risks yourself. If you really desire to be better and beat the the average, be in charge of your happiness as well as your life.

Make the risk of breaking From Their Comfort Zone Are you looking to stand out from the crowd? Try taking a chance and breaking out of your comfortable zone. It doesn't matter if begin with baby steps, what's important is how you start. Being constantly in a state of security you don't have is not will help you improve as a person or even spiritually. Take the chance and do something different and try something different and break away from your usual routine. You may be surprised, and it could be more effective than you ever thought possible.

A Risk-Failure chance that those who have succeeded are willing to take is the risk failing. They're not afraid of take on new challenges.

They are prepared to go for it without worrying that they might be unsuccessful. Even if they fail badly they're not scared to rise up, get their feet back and attempt to take a new risk. People that are prepared to risk it all who can get out of the mediocre life. Don't be afraid to make the leap and rid yourself of the fear of failing There is nothing you aren't able to take on.

The Risk of Letting Go: Finally one of the most successful people living a life above average does not hesitate to give up. They accept the fact that to let new things come in your lifestyle, it is necessary to create space. It's like having a full closet. If you don't clear out things that you don't want or use, you won't find a space to put new items. They let go of the past, their circumstances, or experiences that are no value to them and can move on with confidence.

Therefore, be brave and take a chance to move out of your comfortable zone and be above average. It is meant for life to be enjoyed, enjoyed and, of course, appreciated. If you don't keep your security and safety in mind constantly you're never going to be anything other than normal. One wise person once stated, "Life is too short to wake up every morning regretting your choices. Be grateful for those who treat you well and forget about those who do not. If you are given the chance to do something, make the most of it. If it will change your life, do it. There is no guarantee that it will be easy, but they declared that it was worth the effort."

Chapter 9: Creating A Planning

Reviewing the current situation

If you are looking at your current circumstances to determine if you're on the right path start by determining your priorities, interests abilities, lifestyle, and skills.

Your values determine who you are as well as how you conduct yourself within the community. Understanding what is important to you in the areas of belonging, money to others, helping others, and self-development, for instance is crucial. It's impossible to be content when your present circumstances don't match your ideals.

To be productive and satisfied, you have to be engaged in at least some aspects of your work. Find out what interests you and then assess your current work environment to find out if it has the elements you are interested in.

The suitability of a job depends on how it enhances your abilities. Examine your strengths and weaknesses. are.

Every decision you make in relation to your current circumstances must be based on your ideal lifestyle. You should seek a balance between your personal and professional life.

The job that is right for you

The job that is right for you

Are you working in your dream job? Do you think the profession you've picked is best suited to you? It's not easy to make this decision as it requires lots of self-reflection and evaluation. A lot of people are stuck in unsatisfactory jobs due to the fact that it's difficult to dig into and determine what they actually would like from their career. They're not miserable, but they're certainly not truly content either. It's not necessary to be one of them.

The ideal job doesn't have to be about fame or money It's not always what you imagine to be the "dream career." Consider Silda as an example. She was in the position she always believed was the ideal job. She was earning a hefty salary in a well-known law firm in a major city. The position was prestigious and offered all the cash Silda could ever require. However, something was not quite right. Silda was unhappy most often.

A few days ago, Silda was assigned to an open-ended case involving families with low incomes and a shady landlord. When she worked with the family Silda discovered her passion She loved helping people.

After some hard contemplation, Silda quit her job and joined the public Defender's Office. She is now helping people who are struggling to navigate the legal system. She earns less than she did before, yet she's never been happier.

As Silda When you look at your current circumstances it is necessary to take a deep soul-searching. You'll need to ask yourself some hard questions like: Are satisfied with what you're doing? Do you have the ability to make changes which will enable you to be content with your current position or do you need to look for a new job?

In this section we'll look at some of the factors you should be aware of in order to be able to respond. These include your values, preferences, abilities and lifestyle you'd like to live. When taken together, all of these aspects will help you decide if your current circumstances are suitable for you or if you're in need of making adjustments.

While you are studying this article, you should take an outline of your personal preferences, values, hobbies and aspirations for the future. Your list will help you assess your personal circumstances.

What are your values?

What are you most proud of?

What is the most important thing to you? Money? Family? Status? Your values, your beliefs, principles and beliefs - are a reflection of who you are and decide how you react to the events. They're also a significant aspect of whether you're doing the right thing or not.

How do your values connect to your work? If your job is in line with your values, then you're at the right place for you. However, if your work demands you to perform actions which are against your beliefs then you're not going to be satisfied. Think about two colleagues who are Ree or Evan.

Ree as well as Evan both are in high-pressure environments. Choose one of them to find out more about the ways in which their values determine their satisfaction with their jobs.

Ree

Ambition and money are two of Ree's most important values. She is awed by the challenges of working in a high-pressure setting which gives her an opportunity to grow quickly as well as a huge pay raise. Ree is thrilled with her current position.

Evan

Evan is unhappy. Evan's primary concern is family. primary value. The pressure-filled environment and the need to work weekends and overtime cause him to be stressed.

While Evan loves his pay, he'd much rather be working a regular schedule or weekends with no work. Actually, Evan is starting the process of reviewing his current job situation to figure out if there is a way to improve his situation, or if he should seek a new job.

These values are: the family, money, self-development belonging, autonomy, and ambition to name only the most important. Many people share the same values, however the mixture of values and preferences is different to each person. It is possible to determine the most important values in your life by asking several key questions.

Money

What is important to you the fact that you are earning lots of cash? Do you think it is worth the sacrifice of other aspects, like friends and family time such as, say, a family dinner?

Family

What is the most important thing spending time with your loved ones? If it is necessary, are willing to sacrifice other matters, such as cash and a top-quality job?

Self-development

Do you need to keep learning new techniques and expand your mind?

Being a part of

Do you maximize your relationships with friends and family at work? Are you most satisfied working in an environment that promotes the sense of community?

Autonomy

What is the importance of being able to work in a team, free of interruption from peers or supervisors?

Ambition

Do you think it is important that you accelerate your career and gain the respect of other colleagues?

The importance of asking these questions is. It can help you understand your values that are most important to you and help determine whether you're in the right career. If not, it's much easier to make a change sooner rather than waiting until you're stuck in a path to work that isn't a good fit for you.

What are your hobbies?

What are your hobbies?

As well as finding your core values in your life, evaluating your current circumstances will require you to be into the things which you enjoy or "ring the bell." What are your hobbies?

It's amazing that so many people have jobs they're not at all. Yvette is able to make it to work every single day however she doesn't have any motivation for her work. Although she's talented, her focus isn't on her work, and she's not performing well. Her work will not last for long-term.

Compare this with Daniel who is a lover of his job. He's always enthusiastic and eager to be the best he can be. He's also very creative and has great ideas for his company. Daniel is extremely efficient.

Question

Finding your interests is much easier than you imagine. Hobbies, for instance will help you pinpoint your passions.

What other aspects do you think will aid you in determining the areas you're interested in?

Options:

1. Activities you enjoy

2. You enjoyed subjects at your school

3. There are jobs that could entice you.

4. Industries that could entice you

5. People you like

6. You've had fun watching movies

Answer

Things you like, subjects you enjoyed during school, occupations that you might be interested in and fields that could appeal to you are four ways to determine your interests.

Many factors can help you pinpoint your interests. These include classes, activities and jobs that look appealing, and even industries that look appealing.

Activities

What experiences at work and in your personal life you've had over the past few years that you truly liked? Are these adventures mostly adventure-related or more intellectual? Do they all have the same passion? Do they all match to what you currently do to earn your livelihood?

The subjects of school

What were your top subjects at high school? Did you enjoy the sciences, math, art as well as foreign languages? What activities outside of school were you most interested in?

Jobs

Are there specific tasks that you are interested in? Perhaps you'd like the position of an interior decorator, web designer, music teacher or a landscape gardener, for instance.

Industries

Are there any specific industries that you are interested in? Maybe you'd like to research manufacturing, advertising electronics, health care teaching, entertainment, or even entertainment.

When thinking on your hobbies, you should be cautious not to mix the things you're interested in with the things you're skilled at. They're not always identical. Don't fret if you do not have any burning or all-consuming interest. Few people do. Spend the time to think about what you like, and reduce it to the things that really interest you.

What do you excel at?

What are you skilled at?

In addition to your values and passions, you must also to define your talents and then answer the question "What are my strengths?" The majority of skills are of two kinds that are hard and soft abilities.

Hard skills

The skills that are hard to master tend to be specific and specialized to the occupations they are used in. For instance, being able to operate an application for word processing is not an easy skill as is being able to drive a car, create white sauce, or take part in a game.

Soft skills

Soft skills can be easily transferred. They're not a prerequisite for any occupation. For instance, the ability to solve difficult problems, have open-minded, communicate well and clearly, be able to manage multiple tasks at once and be attentive are all soft abilities.

The best questions in determining your strengths are based on your abilities. They cover your capacity to perform a variety of tasks:

* organize work,

* collaborate with others,

* handle multiple projects simultaneously,

* find solutions to problems * resolve problems

* can communicate effectively.

There's a second important question which can help you evaluate your strengths Do you have potential areas that aren't fully explored? A lot of people have abilities and strengths aren't yet fully developed.

For example, Juan is good with youngsters and loves working with youngsters. He could be a great teacher. to be an excellent teacher.

What kind of life style do you desire?

What type of lifestyle do you desire?

You've been working on identifying your priorities, interests and abilities. However, these aren't the only things to consider when looking at your current circumstances. Before you make any decision about your circumstances, you need to consider your lifestyle requirements.

Everyone requires food clothes, shelter and food for just the essentials. Your ability to acquire the basic necessities and the other items you may require, is directly influenced by the results you receive from your job. Even when money isn't a top priority to you, money is an important factor to consider. In essence, you must have enough money to cover your requirements.

However, money isn't everything. What's the deal with health insurance? Disability and life insurance? A pension? A severance plan? These "extras" could make your life manageable, and can be vital to your family and you. A lot of companies offer some or even all these advantages as part of your compensation plans.

Alongside compensation and benefits, it is important to consider other aspects of your life including the ability to plan personal time, holidays vacation time, travel demands and the where you live.

Time for personal time

Are you able to make the time to schedule time off to manage pressure and responsibilities for example, taking care of children or your elderly parents?

Holidays

Do you have the ability to take important holidays off? for example, Christmas Kwanzaa, Ramadan, or Yom Kippur as an example?

Time for vacation

Are you able to take enough time off to relax and enjoy time with your loved ones?

Travel requirements

What amount of travel will the job requires? Does this create a problem for your family members? Can travel advances be arranged to ensure that you don't need to travel on your own cash?

Location

Are you located in the region in which you'd like to be? If your job requires you to relocate will the expenses be paid? Are you concerned that relocating could negatively affect your family?

In the end, you must seek to strike a equilibrium between your family and work Find an employment opportunity that permits flexibility. Flexible working options such as flexible hours, part-time work or job sharing as well as telecommuting are available from a number of businesses. These options allow you to have more control over your time and the way you live your life. However, they do require sacrifices.

If, for instance, you require a reduction in your work hours to accommodate your family obligations, you could be required to negotiate a lesser amount of pay or find the job with less

Responsibility and lower standing. If you choose to work at your home, you run the danger losing access to crucial channels of communication.

Find out what is important to you and what you'd like to achieve and what you're willing to give up in order to attain it. Determine how you can make the best working conditions for you.

Question

When you are evaluating your job, what are the most important questions to ask yourself?

Options:

1. What are my values?

2. What are my hobbies?

3. What are I skilled at?

4. What kind of lifestyle do you wish to live or do I want to live?

5. Who will I be able to mentor?

6. What can I do to help me advance rapidly?

Answer

1. This choice is true. Knowing your values allows you to choose a path that is in line with the person you are.

2. This one is the best option. If you're keen on the aspects in your position, you'll feel satisfied.

Third Option: The third choice is the correct one. Learn about what your weaknesses and strengths are. Your abilities determine the kind of job you're best suited to.

Fourth option: The fourth choice is the correct one. Any choice you make with regard to your personal situation should be considered in relation to your life goals.

Option 5 It's a bad choice. Knowing who will be the mentor for you won't aid in determining the situation appropriate for you.

Option 6 It is a bad choice. If you consider ambition to be one of your most important values, then learning how to move quickly may be an option for you. In other words, it will not assist you in evaluating your work.

How to determine your strengths and weaknesses

If you're thinking of making a change in your career it is important to be in a position to leverage your strengths in areas where your skills and interests meet. If you're not sure the areas where you excel and what you are able to do, use feedback from your colleagues and boss to find out about these areas. You can also conduct surveys to determine areas in which you are able and have desire. If you know your strengths, it is possible to strive to build a satisfying career path that leverages your strengths.

Alongside strengths, you should also be aware of your weaknesses. If you don't, they could hinder you from achieving your goals for your career. These are areas of your job that you are unable to meet the minimum requirements. Information sources about the weaknesses you have are your self-evaluation, coworkersand boss. If you are discussing your shortcomings with the boss make sure to plan your responses in advance for the meeting.

If you recognize your weaknesses, you can begin to fix them. If your weaknesses cannot be corrected then you will need to learn how to make them more acceptable.

Recognize your strengths

Find your strengths

Do you recognize your strengths? You ought to. Your strengths are similar to stairs. If you're thinking about moving up in your career your strengths determine whether you're ready to progress to a new job and, in the end will you be content with the job you've been doing.

You can't be proficient at something you don't like or to be attracted to things aren't your forte. You must find the areas in which your talents and interests meet. Your strengths are in these areas. When your work is a good use of your strengths, a variety of other aspects of your life - work satisfaction as well as motivation and satisfaction for example - will all fall into the right place.

Two employees leverage their strengths to fulfill tasks. Vishruti and Telly each work for an insurance firm which includes Vishruti as supervisor within Quality Assurance, and Telly as a project manager within the Marketing Department. Both employees are aware of their strengths and utilize these strengths to search for opportunities to advance their careers.

Vishruti

Vishruti is the chair of the committee for process improvement. She is extremely satisfied by her work on the committee as it allows her to blend her skills in the field of quality assurance and her desire to work in an team with other people.

Telly

Telly is on a short-term assignment in the Actuarial Department. This allows him to use his management skills for project management along with his love of math. Because he's proficient at the work and enjoys working in this way, he receives the respect he seeks.

Professionals are generally aware of the strengths they have, so you might be able to determine what your strengths are. Feedback from colleagues and family members and appraisals of performance from your supervisors are both good source of data.

It is also possible to discover your strengths through surveys or questionnaires.

The sample survey contains an activity list, as well as columns to determine what the activities are. a passion or has an aptitude. A checkmark in both the interest section and in the Abilities segment for an exercise indicates that the activity is an area of strength.

Did you make a list similar to what you may have thought to be your strengths?

One benefit having a clear understanding of your talents is you're more in deciding on an occupation that provides satisfaction and fulfillment.

While your strengths lie in areas where your talents and interests meet, it's typically your interests that outweigh your strengths when deciding on the profession you'll take on. For instance, Dan is good at mathematical analysis and financial analysis however he'd probably be miserable being an accountant. Dan's true passion is spending time outdoors and helping to protect the habitat of animals. Dan's passion is enough to make him want to take on a job in conservation.

Question

Kyle is working to identify his strengths. Based on the results of his survey What are his strengths?

Kyle was screened through teamwork, tools coaching or training fellow workers, as well as making use of technology to help others. He has checked his skills with tools, leadership skills and initiative, as well as mentoring and instructing others, as well as making use of technology to enhance his skills.

Options:

1. Utilizing tools

2. Teamwork

3. Leadership

4. Inspiring

5. The process of mentoring and training others

6. Making decisions

7. Making use of technology

Answer

Choice 1: The first choice is the correct one. This is a talent and a passion, so it's an asset.

Option 2. This is a bad choice. This is an interest, but not a capability, therefore it's not an attribute.

Option 3 The wrong choice. This is a skill, but it's not an interest which is why it's not considered an advantage.

Fourth option: The fourth choice is not correct. This is an ability, but it's not an interest, which means it's not a strong point.

Alternative 5: The choice is the correct one. It's an interest and skill, therefore it's an asset.

Option 6 is a wrong choice. It's not a strength, it's neither an interest nor a talent.

7. This choice is the correct one. This is a strength, it's an interest as well as the ability.

Find your weak points

Find your weak points

Alongside being aware of your strengths, you must also be aware of your weaknesses. The advantage of being aware of those weaknesses will ensure that they will not suddenly surface to hinder your efforts and hinder you from achieving your professional objectives.

What is the definition of a weakness? In particular, a weakness refers to an area that isn't meeting the minimum requirements required for an occupation.

You may, for instance, not have the necessary knowledge or skills required to perform the job. Your knowledge of technology may be outdated. You may not be able to manage the inevitable conflicts in the workplace.

Education or training is not available.

If you're considering a change in your job or grow in your career, you'll be in

Competition with others. There are some who possess better abilities, higher training, or even a greatereducational background than you are. Insufficient training or education can be corrected, so make sure that you take care to correct this flaw.

Expertise in technology is out of date

It is essential to keep up-to-date on the latest technologies within your industry and within your workplace. It's also a challenge - technology evolves constantly. The good thing is that it's easy to find resources for training technologies-related abilities.

Unable to handle conflicts

People tend to avoid confrontation. Maybe they are afraid to lose their temper and lose control at the workplace. Maybe they're scared of anger in itself. If you're not able to cope conflicts, certain tasks and jobs will take a lot of effort for you to complete, for example, working as an entire team, working with people, or even directly working for the boss.

Do not let weaknesses keep you from progressing and hinder your progress, you must address these weaknesses face-to-face. This is a two-step procedure. The first step is to identify your weak points. After that, you work on those you can.

To find weaknesses, get information from three main sources: your colleagues, and finally, your boss.

You

You might already have an idea of what you'll must know, master and master. Examine the job description and evaluate the quality of your performance on each job. Examine your performance appraisal for any suggestions on weak points or areas that could be improved.

Coworkers

The perspective of your coworkers is different that you have about your strengths or developmental needs. Get a trusted colleague to provide you with some advice on this.

Boss

The most beneficial feedback about your weak points could be by your manager. It is possible to put off your next performance evaluation to get information about these weaknesses or arrange an appointment with your boss right now. Be proactive and you'll be better than waiting.

If you plan to sit down in front of your manager to talk about your issues You must be prepared for the meeting thoroughly. The first step is to schedule a time where the boss isn't overly stressing and give sufficient time to discuss the issue that is at minimum 30 minutes.

Then, as you discuss Be sure to keep these guidelines in your mind:

• State the reasons you are bringing to the discussion. They should be able to address your desire to improve yourself and provide an explanation of how you appreciate your boss's insight on your performance.

* Make sure you clarify any statements made by your bosses that aren't transparent to you. Request clarification for general assertions, like "You're too disorganized" or ask examples.

* Don't get defensive. Be attentive to the criticisms of your boss. If you don't agree with something mentioned, you can investigate in the future, but don't act in a negative way.

* Recognize and then summarize as you go to ensure you are understanding.

* End with a positive note, taking a vow to improve and thanking your boss for his contribution.

Kumar plans the appointment of Linda his boss to discuss his shortcomings. He schedules an appointment following lunch, and before the afternoon appointment. He ensures that he requests one hour off of her schedule. Be sure to follow along and consider how the Kumar is following the guidelines of discussion.

Kumar I would like to thank you for having me meet, Linda. I would like to speak with you about the weak points that hinder me from progressing. I appreciate your opinion and would like to hear your opinions about how I can make improvements.

Kumar says

Linda Linda: Thank you for your affirmation of your confidence Kumar. In reality, the only weak point I believe you should be focusing on is organization skills. We can discuss more about this in the annual assessment.

Linda says

Kumar The review doesn't have a date for the next three months, but I'd like to begin improving my process immediately. Could you provide me with examples of where I'm not organized?

Kumar asks

Linda: Sure. This week, you didn't have any idea of where your team was working on this project of serial integration. I've been asked three times to provide copies of the standards of the project.

Linda is stern with her words.

Kumar"I've been doing two different projects simultaneously This is the reason I've been somewhat unfocused lately.

Kumar says, defensively

Linda Then that's not an acceptable answer, Kumar. You requested this meeting, remember did you not?

Linda says brusquely

Kumar: I apologize. It's true. I have to work on my organization skills and I'm capable of doing that. Thank you for your comments.

Kumar says

Linda: You're welcome. I'm impressed that you've taken the initiative to improve your performance.

Linda says

Kumar made a mistake in his conversation with Linda she was a bit rude and fell out of control. It's normal to try to defend yourself from criticism, you must keep your eyes on the ball. Remember, the feedback your boss gives you is valuable even if it's difficult for you to comprehend. It's essential if you want trying to improve your weaknesses.

Take care of your weak points

Take care of your weak points

It can be difficult to accept the information you receive about your shortcomings and weaknesses, but you'll never be able to make improvements until you understand what they are. After you've identified your weaknesses that you're not aware of, you can formulate an action plan to address them.

You can improve your deficiencies in areas of soft skills like spoken and written communication delegation, interpersonal, and written skillsby attending classes in the classroom or online. It is also possible to ask your coworkers to assist in editing your memos or reports when you aren't sure about accuracy.

It is possible to correct any weak points in areas that require hard-skills, such as technical skills, by undergoing the same types of training that you receive for soft abilities. Furthermore to that, the Web is a great source of information regarding the most recent technical capabilities.

Take a look at the way Clara quickly takes action to fix her flaws. Clara struggles with keeping her schedule in order. She was told by her boss that her poor time management could be the reason for her weaknesses. Clara's workplace doesn't have a training facilities and, therefore, Clara looks up resources on the internet. She registers for an online course on time management which meets her requirements.

In a determined effort to address her weaknesses in time management, Clara was able to fix it fairly quickly. Indeed time management became one of her strengths.

Question

Lila recently got her annual performance appraisal. The weaknesses she had were highlighted as lack of presentation in accuracy, as well as interpersonal skills.

What do you think Lila do to combat her weakness?

Options:

1. Request suggestions from her boss regarding how she can make improvements

2. Learn online on presentation skills.

3. Have a coworker proofread your the reports before you submit the reports.

4. Take part in a class about dealing with various personalities to enhance your interpersonal abilities

5. Volunteer for tasks that require her to give presentations to the entire organization.

6. Request opportunities to interact with customers

Answer

1. This choice is true. Clara's boss is a great source of information on weaknesses and the best ways to deal with the weaknesses.

2. This one is the correct one. Participating in training classes is an the most effective method to overcome the weaknesses.

Third option: The third choice is the correct one. A coworker who is able to edit written documents is a great method to correct accuracy issues like grammar and spelling errors.

4. This choice is the correct one. Lila could increase her social skills by taking a class that includes roleplaying included.

Option 5 The wrong choice. Lila must improve her presentation skills before she is able to volunteer to give presentations for the entire company. In other words, she's showing a flaw.

Option 6 It is a wrong choice. Lila should work on the interpersonal abilities of her before using them to deal with customers.

Question

You now understand the importance of identifying your strengths and weaknesses.

What are the advantages from doing this?

Options:

1. If you recognize your strengths, it is possible to pursue a fulfilling job that makes use of the strengths you have.

2. If you're not aware of the weaknesses you have, it will stop you back from reaching your goals in life.

3. If you aren't aware of your strengths, you won't be successful.

4. If you recognize your weaknesses, you'll be successful.

Answer

1. This one is the correct one. When a skill and an interest meet with each other, you've got a strong. If you're able utilize your strengths, you're more productive in your job.

2. This one is the correct one. Insufficiencies - defined as the failure to satisfy the minimum requirements for the job - can keep you back. If you are aware of your weaknesses, you are able to focus on overcoming them.

Option 3. This is not the best option. You could be successful if you don't know your strengths, however you're probably not going to be content at work.

Option 4 It is a bad choice. For success it is essential to work on your mistakes, not be aware of them.

Setting Your Career Goals

Once you've assessed your situation and have a complete list of your goals, values, needs strengths, weaknesses, and needs then you must pull the pieces together and formulate your career strategy. It can be accomplished with three easy steps.

It is the first thing to create your vision for the future. This is your long-term goal for your career. When you design your plan, make sure you are real and honest. Be aware of your personal values, interests as well as your strengths and weaknesses. You can then conduct some market research to figure out what you need to do to achieve your goal.

Once you have formulated your dream It is important to decide how you can get there and create your plan of action. Determine what skills and experience you'll need to obtain. Find out the resources available to assist you in getting this information and experiences.

Last, establish a time line for your development plan. It should include the responsibility of reviewing the plan's content. This will allow you to maintain your plan when you and the environment evolve over time.

Create a vision for the future

Make a plan for the future

Once you've assessed your current situation and have a comprehensive list of your needs, values strengths, weaknesses and priorities then you must pull everything together and create your career strategy.

The process of planning your career includes three steps: first, you must create an idea of what the future will look like and then create an action plan, and finally, develop an action plan for achieving your objectives.

Have you ever encountered an interviewer, supervisor or manager ask you the well-known question "So what do you envision for your self in five years?" Did you come up with a convincing answer? Are you paralyzed as a deer caught in headlights?

If you're not able to give a clear response to the question above, then you aren't able to create a vision to your next step. Without a plan it is possible that you will find yourself in a dead-end position or in a string of jobs that end up being disappointing.

If you've got a goal however, you could aim at specific tasks and tasks, which could serve as steps to help you get the direction you'd like to take.

Your vision is your ultimate career objective, your primary direction. If you decide to create your vision, you need to keep the following important aspects in your head:

Be honest with yourself and remember your interests, values and lifestyle goals, your strength and weak points, as well as your personal qualities.

Don't be too committed to a particular career or path. Your life circumstances will change over time, and you'll evolve as well as you go through your life and encounter new experiences.

* Don't get caught up with the details. Keep your eyes on the bigger picture and don't worry about the minute details.

If you have ever dreamed of the future, you may have asked yourself a few questions to spark your imagination. These kinds of questions will help you clarify your ideals What is a specific subject or activity that I like? Do I have a specific job that is appealing to me? Is there a particular industry that I'd like to explore?

Do you have a favorite thing or topic that I find enjoyable?

It's not easy to turn an passion into a job However, you can't be able to enjoy your career when you don't pursue the things you're passionate about. Make use of your interests or the things you like to form your dream.

Do you know of a specific job that I am interested in?

If you've always wanted become a firefighter, contractor, or even an actuary, it's the right time to seriously think of becoming one. You don't want to be looking at 20 years from now, regretting that you did not pursue an occupation you really loved.

Is there a particular industry I'd like to research?

You might be thinking about working for an insurance company or perhaps you're drawn to aerospace companies or engineering industry. Consider what you've got to offer, what kind of job that you'd get and the kind of work you'd do.

It's an excellent idea to conduct market research in order to confirm that the job you want to pursue actually exists. You want to discover the right market or sector in which you can realize your dream most effectively.

Begin by looking at your current workplace and think about the areas that might have an need for your talents. How do your strengths work in these areas? And what types of problems can you solve for the company?

Think about whether any changes are happening that could affect your outlook. For instance, if interested in the field of health insurance and it is experiencing changes in the way it operates Consider figuring out what these changes will mean for your outlook for the future.

If you're not sure that you'll succeed in achieving your dream in the current market, you should research different markets. Utilize all sources to find out more details. The Internet is particularly useful. It is also possible that you would like to begin developing a network with whom you can exchange information about your job.

Question

Lauren is currently employed as an adjuster for claims at the insurance firm. Her strong abilities in maths have helped her secure her position, but Lauren isn't planning to stay an adjuster for very long.

Lauren is extremely determined and ambitious. Status and wealth are very important to Lauren's life. Lauren's strengths are administration, leadership, the initiative and making decisions. Lauren is weak in the area of negotiation with tools, negotiating, and making use of technology.

Lauren studies her current position. She finds that numerous jobs are available within the company where her skills can be used to great advantage.

What vision of the future will be the best basis for Lauren's career plans?

Options:

1. Within a couple of decades, Lauren becomes an officer of the Finance Division of her company

2. Lauren receives a lateral transfer and becomes proficient in setting premiums for insurance groups.

3. Lauren decides to go off by herself and eventually becomes the chief executive officer of a high-tech business

Answer

Option 1 Option 1: This is the best choice. Lauren's mathematical abilities as well as her determination and her strengths can easily propel her in this direction.

Option 2. This is a bad choice. While Lauren is likely to use her math abilities to set group rates A lateral transfer isn't exactly in line with Lauren's values and ambitions.

Option 3 This is a bad alternative. This idea would be logical when technology was Lauren's strength. But the truth is that technology is weak point.

Decide how to realize your goals

Decide how to realize your goals

Lauren has set out her plan. She has set a huge and challenging target. She now has to determine how she can achieve her goal, and create a plan of action for achieving it.

How do you navigate to places you've never visited before? By using a map, of course. When you're on your professional path constantly expanding your horizons. To keep yourself safe from known dangers and also to safely reach your destination you require a action plan.

A plan of action is a precise outline of your goals and goals you have to reach in order to attain your vision.

When you've created your plan of action it's easier to break the timeline into manageable chunks, and then work from the beginning point forward. No one can think fifteen years into the future, because there are too many factors to take into consideration. But you can think about where you would like to be in a year from right now.

In many ways the process of action planning is like the appraisal process. It is a process of determining the direction you'd like to go or what you would like to achieve one year from now to achieve your career objective. Then , you set shorter-term goals and targets that will lead you to where you want to be.

Why should you bother creating goals and goals? If you don't take the time you'll forget about your progress. It's possible to lose track of your goal. Objectives and goals allow you to mark off the skills you require in the process of acquiring these. They give you a sense of growth that will last for the long run and encourage you to stay in your journey.

Short-term objectives and targets are set to address any deficiencies in your knowledge and skill levels.

Certain deficiencies may be due to the lack of knowledge. For example, do you require to know more about specific subject areas? Do you need to learn about the HR policies of your business? The answer to knowledge deficits is to train. Some deficiencies may be due to gaps in your experience. Perhaps you'll need to improve your interview techniques or improve your ability to interact with customers. Only you can correct any mistakes made by experiences.

Training

It's not difficult to find resources for training. A lot of organizations have internal training facilities. Local universities and colleges offer classes in a variety of subjects. The Internet is a fantastic resource to find training courses. The Internet can also be a delivery method for online training that can satisfy your requirements in the event that traditional classroom training isn't accessible or practical.

Experience

The process of gaining experience can be a challenge. Like many college graduates who complain, "How can I gain experience if there is no way to hire me without prior experience?" You can get experience in different ways like volunteering, internships, temporary work or job shadowing.

If, for instance, you're interested in humanitarian work then you could volunteer at an orphanage or homeless shelter. This lets you find out if you truly enjoy doing this type of work. If you're hoping to sell investments, look for someone willing to let you work with the person for a day in the field. It will provide you with an excellent impression of what the work will be to be "from from the inside."

When you develop your action plans, you must identify the education and experiences that will allow you to be able to meet the demands of your ideal job.

For instance, in order to be an officer within the firm's Finance Division, Lauren will require experience and acquire the MBA, Master of Business Administration. This degree is among the requirements for the job she's aiming for.

Lauren is also required to determine her job skills that she'll require. In this case, she might decide to pursue an opportunity for a transfer lateral in within the Finance Division. Then, she will be able to look into the surrounding environment and begin preparing her route to the top position.

Create a timeline to achieve your goals.

The final step in establishing your career plan is to establish the time line. It is something you should complete while you develop an action plan. It is the timeline that differentiates the action plans apart from basic to-do list. People react to deadlines as they do not want to go over them. Thus, assigning dates to tasks aids in ensuring that the tasks will be completed in the time frame you want.

An action plan may take various types. The one Lauren utilizes has space for her objectives, goals and the steps she must complete to achieve her goals. Alongside each step is an area for dates. Lauren sketches into some tentative dates and then redraws them when she prioritises her actions and tightens her plan.

When she adds dates on the plan Lauren seems close to getting it done, but there's one more thing to complete. She must include the provision to review the plan on a regular basis.

People change over time. The world changes, and priorities shift. If you do not alter your action plan to align with your own personal preferences then the plan ceases be useful and is a relic. To avoid this it is recommended to include "Evaluate the action program" in the form of an objective in the plan, and include an estimated time to complete.

Question

After a year of Lauren's plan her calendar program informs the girl that she needs to review her plan. First, Lauren re- examines her vision. Did it change? Not even a little. Then she thinks about her present situation. It is

changed quite a lot. Lauren's priorities have changed; she's taken the decision to have a baby.

Which action do you believe Lauren will do to address her latest priority?

Options:

1. It is not necessary to take any action

2. Lauren has decided to revoke her plans

3. Lauren will modify her actions and the time line

4. Lauren is planning to create a new strategy that is a reflection of her new priorities

Answer

Option 1 The wrong choice. Although her perspective has not changed her priorities for the immediate future have changed. Lauren needs to alter her time and actions.

Option 2. This is not the right choice. Lauren does not intend to alter her original vision. She'll need to make modifications to certain actions - particularly her timeline.

Option 3 3. This is the best choice. Lauren will have to alter her schedule and her time line to allow for the time needed to begin the family.

Option 4 The incorrect choice. Lauren isn't required to develop an entirely new plan. She simply needs to modify her existing strategy to accommodate her changing goals.

Lauren's outlook hasn't changed. She's still set to become the chief of the Finance Division. To accommodate her new role, Lauren needs to make some real-world changes to her plans. Lauren decides to allow her time to reach her goal.

In other words, instead of having to be a full-time employee and take on the full load of courses, like she is currently, Lauren becomes a part-time student. It takes her longer to get her MBA however, it will also allow her the time to spend with her family.

Re-examining her plan and revising it in accordance with the current circumstances Lauren's plan is an essential tool to help her to stay on track towards achieving her goals.

Chapter 10: Start Going On The Right Track
Job Opportunities Within Your Organization

Whatever your goals for your career you should take the time to look into your options is a good idea as you cannot depend on getting an opportunity to be promoted. One of the most effective places to look for opportunities to develop the career path is inside your company.

You could look for a change in your job within your workplace in various ways, but three most popular methods are to identify opportunities, pursuing opportunities for professional development as well as considering an lateral move.

You can successfully make an internal job shift

Making your career Autopilot, and then letting it lead you wherever it will is simple. However, once you've accomplished those goals, then it could be time to leave your familiarity zone. At some point you'll decide that it's time to seek the next step in your career or accept more responsibility.

Every once in a while you ought to consider exploring your options for career advancement. In the current business environment you shouldn't be expecting an automatic promotion

. You'll be required to aid to move the process forward. One of the most effective places to look for opportunities to boost you career path is in your business.

Moving roles within your company

You may request a job shift within your business in a variety of ways, but here 3 are among the more commonly used:

1. Find opportunities

2. Look for professional opportunities for development

3. Consider a lateral move

Find opportunities

The first step to an efficient in-house job shift is to look for potential opportunities and jobs that could be offered within your company.

Look for internal announcements

A majority of businesses offer a job advertisement program. This may be a physical bulletin board or an online section.

Find out when jobs are advertised and make certain to review the job jobs listings for the days. Be sure to check frequently - if you don't check in on a particular day, you may miss out on a fantastic chance.

Be aware of the company's rules

You should be aware of the company's rules regarding the procedure for job changes Both formal and informal rules. Each company has its own rules. For example, your business might require you to wait for a year before being permitted in to be considered for an interview for the next position.

There are informal rules too. For instance, some jobs could be filled based on the seniority of the applicant or prior experience with another department.

Request informational interviews

One of the best ways to find possibilities within your company is to schedule informational interviews with those who be aware of the specifics of the job.

If your coworker, Michael, holds the job you'd like. You can talk to him to learn what you'll require in terms of experience and experience to perform the job.

You've viewed the internal job listings and become acquainted with the regulations, and talked to several people on possible avenues you could consider. It's time to utilize the visual representation - - or map - of your business to map the possibilities.

Yvette is an administrator for a major cruise line. She is determined to rise in the company and has discovered a few opportunities to consider. Yvette makes use of an organization chart in order to outline the possibilities. She's fascinated by Marketing and was told that she has lots of good suggestions, and so points to possibilities for the Marketing as well as P.R. Department as a possible option. She's also attending night classes in accounting, which means she's also highlighting her experience in the Finance Department as well.

Seek professional development chances

Seek professional development chances

Question

The second way you can switch jobs within your organization is to look for opportunities to develop your professional abilities.

What do you consider to be examples of opportunities for professional development?

Options:

1. Training in management

2. Certification programs

3. Programs to help students pay for tuition

4. Work colleagues meet after hours to discuss the latest projects

5. Wellness and health programs

Answer

1. This is the correct one. Some companies provide managerial training through their departments of personnel. This is a fantastic method to increase your skills as a professional if you're seeking a managerial job.

2. This choice is the correct one. Many employers assist employees to obtain certificates in particular abilities. This is a great option to develop the professional abilities you require to get a promotion.

3. This choice is the correct one. Employers often provide fees for tuition to classes that are related to their current jobs or positions they may be interested in applying for in the near future.

4. This choice is not correct. Many workplaces encourage employees to socialize and some even offer to pay for social events and events. However, having a meeting with coworkers in the evening to discuss current initiatives isn't a sign of an opportunity for professional growth.

Alternative 5: The choice isn't correct. While a wellness and health program can assist employees in becoming healthier and boost their performance but it's not a method to improve professional abilities.

Finding opportunities for professional development is the second method for changing jobs in the company. This is the process of utilizing every opportunity or resource that could enhance your knowledge.

Apart from management-related training courses as well as certifications or tuition support, the business could also provide training in various management programs, or even leadership. Make sure you learn about all the options offered by your business and avail the ones that are of interest to you.

Naturally, attending courses or classes will help improve your abilities. However, pursuing these opportunities can bring additional benefits:

The fact that you are taking classes shows an interest in learning,

By taking classes, you show you're keen to do more than the minimal requirements for your job and

* if you've invested in your growth, the business is more likely to be looking to

recuperate the cost of development by making you more accountable.

Because Yvette is currently taking classes in accounting at night and is enrolled in the tuition assistance program of her employer. The program reveals that she could receive reimbursement for a part of the expense if her knowledge she gained can be utilized in her job at the firm. The boss is impressed by her efforts, and observes that Yvette is eager to become more responsible. In fact, her boss informs her that once she's finished the course she'll be in a ideal position to move in within the Finance Department.

Consider a lateral move

Consider a lateral move

The last option for an in-house job shift is to contemplate an lateral move. Perhaps you require the right career path that plays to your strengths, or that is pleasing to your motivations. If that's the case, then a transfer lateral to your department or to a different department could be a viable choice for you.

You might even consider taking a demotion. You might be thinking "But isn't that the same as sabotaging your career?" But it's not always. Sometimes, a demotion can place you in the best position to realize your career goals , by placing you on a path that is more compatible in your skills and your values.

It is also advisable to take a moment to ask yourself a few questions. Knowing the answers can aid you in deciding whether a lateral option is the best option.

Why could a lateral shift be the best option for me?

The possibility of switching jobs with the same employer and in the same salary range could aid in expanding your knowledge and knowledge.

That makes you an valued employee, and could boost the security of your job. This also makes you more marketableand with more expertise, in case circumstances don't go your way for you at the current workplace.

Can a lateral change have a negative impact on me?

A lateral movement can have a positive impact on your life when you utilize it to help you develop your long-term plan and gain from your experiences.

Transferring to a different department may provide new opportunities and help you understand how other aspects of business work and perform, both of which are benefits that can enhance your chances of advancing in your career.

How can I keep on the right path?

Before making a lateral decision, you must be aware of whether making a lateral move could place you in the wrong direction in the company you work for.

Examine the top-ranking members of your organisation. Do they have their rank by working for a long time in one particular department? Did they achieve this through gaining experience in a variety of aspects of the business's operations? If the former happens, then a change in direction is unlikely to hinder you from staying on the right path.

When you have a satisfactory answer on these issues, it is time to look at your motives in the context of the possibility of a move to the other side. So, what are the motives behind your decision to choose this route?

For example, perhaps you're taking classes to increase your professional standing and require an easier job. Maybe your family obligations will require you to accept work that is less prone to requirements for travel.

Whatever you are motivated by, identifying these will make it easier to evaluate any possibilities that occur to you.

If you are considering the possibility of a lateral move, bear in mind other crucial aspects: your company's policies on employment and growth areas that could be a possibility, and the odds of success or failure at the job you are considering such as.

Phyllis who was a claims examiner discovered she was not on the right route to reach her goals. She was able to analyze health insurance claims but rarely had a face-to-face meeting with clients who she enjoyed working with. She initially considered moving to an administrative job in order to spend more time with clients. After having a look around she realized that this decision would not keep her career on the right path.

After looking at her options and abilities, Phyllis finally realized that an lateral move is the best option. It won't impact her career negativelyand would allow her to pursue what she truly loves and that is working with other people.

At the end of the day, Phyllis made a lateral transfer into the sales department as an agent for service. She's now happier in her work as well as in a good place to pursue promotions within the Sales Department.

Question

Harry is not happy with his current position, however Harry is happy with the company which he's employed for. Harry is ready to look for a new job with the same organization.

Which strategies could Harry employ to ensure an in-house job transition that is successful?

Options:

1. See the job ads of his employer to find opportunities that align with his interests and skills.

2. Make use of the company's tuition assistance to enroll in a class that is related to the position he's aiming for.

3. Think about a change of job within the department he is currently working in.

4. Be aware of the job advertisements of his company by checking them every month

5. Do not consider an lateral move since such moves usually place employees on a slow pace

Answer

1. This one is the correct one. Many businesses have a formal job-posting program. This could be a bulletin board, or an online space. It is a good way to look for possibilities.

Alternative 2: The second one is the correct one. Finding opportunities for professional development is taking advantage of any possibilities or opportunities that can improve your professional skills.

Third option: The third one is the correct one. A lateral move can be the best option for you when you are looking for career options that play to your strengths or is satisfying your primary motivations.

4. This isn't correct. It is important to know the dates when new job openings are advertised and make sure you check the job listings for the days. Make sure you check them frequently - if you don't check an entire day, you may miss out on a fantastic chance.

5. This choice isn't correct. A lateral move doesn't need to cause your career to go on the back burner. Actually, it may provide you with new contacts and help you understand how other areas of the business operate that are both advantages that can improve your prospects for advancement.

Planning a Promotional Plan

If you're hoping to get promoted or take on more responsibility It's your responsibility to devise a plan of how you'll ensure that your career stays on the right track. This is called your plan for promotion.

Making a plan for promotion will help you in a variety of ways. It will be easier to achieve your goals easily if you integrate your motivational factors into your strategy. You'll stand a greater chance of reaching your goals if you request assignments that are in line with the plan you have laid out. Also, having a plan for promotion ensures that you don't give your career to chance.

Making and implementing a promotion plan generally comprises four steps: selecting the position or job you'd like to be in, researching the requirements for that job, preparing a development plan based on the weaknesses in your skills and, finally, once you're promoted, communicate your enthusiasm about the position to the person who is the best person who makes the decision.

The benefits of a promotional strategy

Benefits of a marketing program

In the current business environment the majority of employees do not automatically move along a certain career course. If you're looking to get promoted or take the reins of your organization It's your job to devise a plan of how you'll stay on the right track. This is also known as your promotion strategy.

Implementing and creating a successful promotion strategy will help you in a variety of ways:

Your career will not happen because of luck. circumstances,

Your goals will be more easy to accomplish if you've put your motivational factors,

You'll have a greater likelihood of achieving your goals if you know what assignments you should ask for.

The way you work will not be a result of chance

If you have a promotion strategy that is in place you can ensure that your career doesn't be the result of luck events. The direction that you choose to take is yours to decide, and your efforts will be the main reason for your career's path.

The goals will be simpler to reach

One of the most important factors for success lies in motivation and the odds of getting ahead in your career depend on how driven you are. Motivators for you could include accepting new tasks, being able to be proud of your accomplishments, attaining your goals for the future, or meeting specific objectives.

Greater chances of getting goals achieved

With your plan for promotion to guide your career decisions and goals, you'll have a higher chances of reaching your goals if you know what assignments to ask for. Instead of soliciting assignments that may be straightforward or even interesting for you personally it is better to select assignments that can help you along your way.

Take Margo For instance. In the past, she lost her way in her career as a sales rep, never really putting in the effort to advance her career. Then she realized she'd like to get more from her work - she wants to be able to assume more of leadership roles in the near future and so she comes up with an action plan for promotion.

Margo is able to see the benefits instantly. Because she is aware of the job she would like to pursue and can decide on the direction she wants to take in her career. She will take actions to assist her in achieving that goal.

Margo is driven to become an effective sales manager and begins seeking more responsibility. She starts taking on more customers and puts in the effort required to be noticed. Soon, her boss is impressed by her efforts and Margo is confident that she will be promoted to the position she's always wanted.

Question

What are the advantages of having a plan for promotion?

Options:

1. It will be easier to achieve your goals easily if you integrate your motivations into your promotion strategy

2. You'll have a greater likelihood of achieving your goals if you seek assignments that align with your strategy

3. The benefit of having a plan for promotion is that you don't give your career to chance

4. You'll be able to achieve the income you want to earn when you've got a promotion strategy

5. You'll be in a much better chance of receiving an automatic promotion

Answer

1. This one is the correct one. Incorporating motivators to your promotional plan can make reaching your goals more simple, since motivators will provide you with additional incentive.

Alternative 2: The second one is the correct one. You'll be more successful by following a plan which includes the use of both long-term and short-term objectives. It is important to request assignments that can help you attain those objectives.

3. This one is the correct one. The plan you have for your promotion helps you stay focussed on the steps you must perform to ensure your career stays in the right direction.

4. This one is not correct. Promotion plans are beneficial for maintaining your career on the preferred path, however reaching an income threshold isn't a guarantee.

5. This selection is not correct. In the current business climate it isn't common for employees to automatically advance along a particular career direction. If you're hoping to advance in your career it's up to you to devise a strategy for how you'll stay on the right track.

The process of creating a promotional plan

Making a plan for promotion

If you're aware of the advantages of a promotional strategy, you're ready to develop the plan and put it into action. It typically involves four steps. The first step is to select the position or role you'd like to take. Then, you determine what skills are required for the task. Then , you develop a plan that is based on the abilities you don't have. After you've been fully enthusiastic, you communicate an interest to the job to the appropriate individual.

Margo is an sales rep at a firm that offers pharmaceutical supplies. She's currently working on the initial stage of creating an action plan for promotion - selecting the job or role she'd like to be in. Margo has a determination to get promoted. She's decided to look to a position where she'd manage the representatives of a group.

A promotion plan is taking steps in order to reach a certain objective. The best method to determine your goals is to set goals for the job you'd like to be in, just similar to what Margo did in her case.

The next step when creating an effective promotion plan is to determine what you need to know in order to fulfill the job. You need to identify the are the soft and hard skills that you'll require. Because Margo is looking for a job in which she's the leader of an entire team, she's aware that she'll require leadership skills. The job will require a good level of communication and she's added that to her list too.

Question

Are there the most effective ways Margo can determine what's needed for the job or position she's looking for?

Options:

1. You can also speak to those who hold the same position.

2. Look up job descriptions that are posted on the intranet for the company

3. Review the job description for the current position.

4. Contact others who are interested in this position.

Answer

Choice 1: This choice is the correct one. The people who hold the job that you're looking for are great source of info. They will know the qualifications you require to be successful in this job.

Alternative 2: The second one is the correct one. The job descriptions you see on your intranet for your company contain all the details on what qualifications are needed for the position.

Third Option: The third choice is not correct. The job description you're given for the current job doesn't provide any clues of the skills you'll require to be successful in the job you're seeking. However, it can aid you in writing your resume, as you'll likely need to include your skills that you already have.

4. This is not correct. While others who are also interested in the job may have an idea of the qualifications required but they're likely to be as unsure as you .

Understanding the skills required to be successful in the job is essential in order to be able to apply for it. But , the skills you possess are only part of the package. In order to be considered a professional it is also necessary to have personal qualities that go beyond your current job. This includes things like ability to think on your feet, flexibility sensibility and loyalty.

Possessing these personal qualities as well as the abilities required for the job, can make you more visible as a person who is"the "total pack." Margo is conducting a self-evaluation of her promotion strategy and is listing the abilities she believes make her a good candidate for promotion and the ones she's looking to improve.

She's always calm when talking to clientsand coworkers and customers are impressed by her ability to listen. However, she has difficulties asserting herself and taking control. Margo has been working for the business for more than 10 years, and she's adding the years to her resume. She is adept at discovering different methods to attract new clients, however she's not very comfortable with the constant change.

Question

The job Margo is interested in needs someone with good leadership and communication abilities. They should also be flexible and trustworthy and have a good business sense. Based on what you've read about Margo what are the traits she do not have?

Options:

1. Communication skills

2. Leadership skills

3. Flexibility

4. Loyalty

5. Business sense is a must.

Answer

1. This choice isn't correct. Margo is always at ease when she speaks to clients, and both her coworkers and clients are impressed by her ability to listen. This indicates that she has excellent communications skills.

Alternative 2: The second choice is the correct one. Because Margo is often having a hard when it comes to asserting herself and taking the initiative, she must develop her leadership abilities.

Third Option: The third one is the correct one. Margo isn't a great person to deal with changes that is crucial in being flexible worker.

Fourth option: The fourth choice isn't correct. Margo has been working for her employer for more than ten years, which proves she's an extremely loyal employee.

Alternative 5: The choice is not correct. Margo's talent for finding new ways to attract new customers suggests she is a smart business person.

To figure out what's needed to take on the new position You must do like Margo did and make a list of skills and qualifications, as well as the credentials and experiences required for the position you'd like to take. What is it that you will need to get promoted?

Once you have a clear understanding of what is necessary to perform the task then you're ready to move to the next step which is to develop your own development plan that is that is based on the capabilities you don't have. A large portion of your promotion plan should comprise of the steps you must complete to attain the skills that you're lacking.

If you've found weak communication skills as well as a lack of knowledge as areas of weakness these are the areas you'll have to improve.

Question

What are ways do you consider Margo might acquire the abilities she's lacking?

Options:

1. Meet with someone from her organization who can help her decide how to get the certification she requires.

2. Find the experience or training she requires

3. Continue in her current position and pray that she can learn enough to get promoted to the job she would like.

4. Learn from a DVD instructional that explains and illustrates the skills she's lacking

Answer

1. This one is the correct one. If you want to acquire the abilities you do not have you must work with an employee mentor who will assist you on the most effective method to acquire the skills you need.

2. This one is the correct one. The easiest method to gain the knowledge you're lacking is to enroll in a course or find another option to acquire the knowledge you want.

3. This choice is not correct. To develop the skills she's lacking, Margo has to take the initiative to acquire the education and experience she requires to get promoted.

Fourth option: The fourth choice is not correct. While an instructional DVD could help, the techniques could not be taught to the same degree as Margo demands.

You'll remember that Margo discovered that she's not equipped with leadership abilities and flexibility. To improve these skills She first talks with her manager, and he is willing to let her take an upcoming class on leadership. Margo is also a life coach who will teach her strategies to help her be more able to adapt to changing conditions. She incorporates these strategies into her promotion plan and within six months, she develops the necessary skills for promotion.

To obtain the necessary qualifications could take anything from 3 to 6 months or more. Whatever it takes, staying to be a great employee is crucial.

You want to be perceived as professional, trustworthy, and an efficient worker regardless of whether you intend to stay in your current job.

You've decided on the position you'd like to be in, figured out your weaknesses and have worked hard to improve these skills. Now is the time to submit your application to get the job and you must communicate your desire to the appropriate person who will make the final decision.

Margo has completed her leadership course and is more prepared to manage the challenges of change. She's now ready to be promoted which is why she's submitting her resume and cover letter in HRD. Human Resources Department. In the meantime she keeps an watch on job ads and job openings that come up. Margo has a strong group of contacts within the business who keep her up to date regarding any possible changes to the management.

Question

Margo is finally able to have a conversation with Edward who is the director of the Sales Department and the person responsible for recruiting and promotions. She presents him with her resume, made up of a complete list of the jobs she's heldand then goes over the information with him.

Do you believe Margo was on the right track during her meeting?

Options:

1. No

2. Yes

Answer

Margo's resume should include every accomplishment she's had and not just a listing of previous positions. If you want to get elevated, your resume must highlight your achievements, accomplishments and abilities. Margo did something right but she did it by giving the resume to the individual in the process and discussed it together with him.

If you have a meeting an individual who is able to decide whether your promotion is possible, make two things happen to ensure a successful encounter:

1. Make sure your resume is filled with all of your accomplishments . It should not be a mere list of previous jobs. In order to get promoted, your resume must reflect your accomplishments, achievements and capabilities.

* It is also recommended to review your CV with the person who made the decision and clarify any information that is unclear and answering any questions they may be asking.

Question

Imagine that you've worked as an teller at a bank for a couple of years. You're really keen to grow your career, so you decide to develop an action plan for promotion.

Follow the steps you need to follow to develop and implement your strategy.

Options:

A. Choose for a promotion to manager of the office

B. Make sure you have office skills, managerial skills and strong interpersonal abilities

C. Confirm that your workplace skills aren't up-to current and develop a plan to obtain the training you require

D. Watch for an open job, then send your cover and resume to the individual who is in charge of hiring

Answer

Make a decision that you would like being promoted as a manager of office is as the first step. The first step to creating and implementing your plan for promotion is to decide on the job or the position you would like to fill.

Find out if you require managerial skills, office expertise and excellent interpersonal skills is a second priority. When you're putting together and implementing your plan for promotion The next step is to discover the skills required for the position you've selected.

Be aware that your office skills aren't up-to the current standards and develop a plan to obtain the education that you need. This is as the third step. The third step in preparing and implementing your plan for promotion is to formulate a development plan that is based on the weaknesses you have.

Find an opening then, submit you resume with a cover letter and CV to those responsible for hiring. This is the fourth step. If you're ready to be promoted the final step in developing and implementing your promo strategy is to communicate you interest for the job to the person who is the best individual who is the decision maker.

Looking for assignments that can help advance Your Career

Requesting specific assignments could aid your career more than just doing the job that you're handed. However, if your boss doesn't know you'd like them they could pass you by them for these tasks.

If you are deciding to accept the new job, follow three strategies to request it. In the first place, you must be sure to ask for it at the right moment. If you have a meeting the boss with whom you work, concentrate on your achievements. In the end, you have to show your value.

Utilizing these strategies can make you appear as someone with an idea and is willing to do the work to get the goals you have set.

Career-enhancing assignments that can help you can help you advance your career

Work assignments that will help will help your career

Jacob has been working at the same firm for five years. He is able to complete any task that the boss assigns him and always submits it promptly. Chen has been with the same firm for three short years. Chen is willing to request assignments that align with the goals she has established for herself. Which one would you say has the more chance of advancement in their careers?

Chen has a higher chance of making progress on her path than Jacob. Why? In fact, soliciting specific assignments could aid your career more than just doing the job you're assigned.

Assignments could be a way to build your skills and opportunities to acquire new knowledge, or the chance to demonstrate the skills that you don't usually see. For example, perhaps you'd like your boss observe how you've mastered an entirely new kind of software, and you request an assignment that uses the software.

One thing to be aware of is that you could be overlooked for these jobs if your boss has a clear understanding of why you're interested in these assignments.

If you decide to be given an assignment that is new You shouldn't simply walk into the office and ask your boss grant you an assignment.

Instead, you need to employ specific strategies to request assignments:

* contact them at the appropriate moment, for example, when you hear of an opportunity that is in line with your plans,

Focus on your achievements by highlighting what you've accomplished in the past.

Show your worth by showing that you're more valuable in your new position than you do in your current position.

Requesting assignments

Requesting assignments

The most important aspect of achieving your desired results is asking the right time. This is the primary method for soliciting assignments. In order to implement this strategy it is important to think about several aspects - being aware about your timing, avoiding poor timing, taking action quickly, and more.

Keep an eye out

Being aware means staying updated on developments that could result in new assignments that meet your needs. Find assignments and request them before they're approved by the management. At the beginning you might be able to influence the terms of the task.

Be aware of opportunities to deliver something that your business requires. If you are able to provide an entirely new approach to an old issue, or figure out an opportunity to accomplish things more efficiently likely you'll be awarded the job.

Beware of bad timing

Sometimes, the right time is to request an assignment. For instance, if , for example, you've recently received a poor performance assessment that was focused on your shortcomings, this isn't the best time to request. First, you must resolve the issue and then follow up after you've made changes.

Get moving quickly

Fast action means that you contact the person who made the decision immediately when you learn of an assignment being looked at that matches your goals. Inform them of your interest and arrange an appointment to discuss what you're able to contribute to the project.

Do more

Being more consistent can make the difference between being noticed and disappearing in the background. If you are willing to go beyond the requirements your boss will be impressed.

Another way to accomplish more is to take responsibility. Being the one who solves a problem after others have handled it will result in a satisfied client praising your boss.

Question

You're a customer service rep and you've heard about an upcoming team being looked at to join your department. You're considering becoming a team leader role because it will aid you in reaching your goals in your career. You schedule an appointment with your boss Karen.

What is a suitable way to approach Karen regarding the job?

Options:

1. "I'm extremely interested in the team that is being formed. I'm interested to know where you are with your plans to build the team which includes the role of team leader. Maybe I could create an orientation kit for the brand new members of the team."

2. "I'd really want to be part the team. I'm sure my performance review was not perfect

however, I believe I'd be a fantastic group leader."

3. "I'm extremely interested in this team. would like to be given the role of team leader."

Answer

Option 1. This is the right choice. You're asking at the appropriate moment to inquire if the details of the project have been finalized . You can also make your desire known by volunteering for a job that matches your career objectives.

2. This one is not true. Making sure you ask at the right time means that you have to ensure you're timing is correct. If you've recently received a poor performance evaluation this is not the right time to make an inquiry.

Third Option: The third is not correct. While you've expressed your desire to be considered for the job but you're not sure whether you're asking at the appropriate moment. Be informed of any assignments that could meet your needs and make sure you request assignments prior to the time the management has them finalized.

Your meeting is scheduled to discuss the task at a suitable time. Now, you should concentrate on your achievements and this is the second method. Focus on what you've accomplished and connect those accomplishments to the things you're hoping to accomplish in your new position. This is about pitching yourself to your boss, possibly by presenting a current resume. Your aim should be to market yourself. Be aware that being your business's most productive employee does not have any significance if nobody else in an authority position is aware of it.

Question

Your boss has asked you, Karen, about the task. Now you're looking to prove to her how your efforts will be beneficial to the formation of the new team.

What would you tell people to be focused on your achievements?

Options:

1. "I am the best customer satisfaction scores in the department . I also have great interpersonal abilities. These skills will be even more valuable in the event that I'm promoted to the position of team leader."

2. "As you've stated before in my performance reviews, I'm a great people, organizational and communication abilities."

3. "Of all the employees within that department, that I'm the best qualified."

Answer

1. This choice is the correct one. You must highlight what you've accomplished, and then sell yourself to your bossby showing how your skills and accomplishments you've had in your current job are relevant to the work you'll do for the new position.

2. This is not correct. Concentrating on your achievements means emphasising your accomplishments and talents and linking them to the new task. People, organizational and communication abilities are valuable however they aren't achievements.

Third Option: The third choice is not correct. You must highlight your achievements, and that means pitching yourself in front of your manager. Your aim should be to make yourself more attractive.

The last strategy to be successful in soliciting the assignment you want is to prove your value. You've made the sale by convincing the person making the decision that you're more valuable in the new task than the work you're currently assigned to do.

One way to accomplish this is to highlight the strengths that aren't being used in your current work that could become relevant in your new job. You could, for instance, take on a task that showcases your skills to be successful in a new job.

Be careful not to oversell yourself in the current situation. You need to present an argument that is convincing for where you are in the event that you aren't able to get the job you're seeking.

Question

You've questioned Karen about the task and discussed your expertise. However, Karen is worried that you're in a bad spot in the moment, because your abilities aren't being used to their fullest potential.

What would you tell Karen to show your relative worth?

Options:

1. "I believe that I'm contributing to a high degree as evident my ratings for customer service. But I also have management and organizational skills could be useful when I'm responsible for creating the team."

2. "Maybe I'm in a bad situation right now. My talents aren't being utilized. This is why it would be better to have me take on this new job."

3. "I believe I'm not in the wrong spot. But I do think I'd do great in the new job."

Answer

1. This choice is the correct one. To show your worth, demonstrate you'd be more valuable in your new position than your colleagues, but don't sell yourself short of your current position.

2. This choice is not correct. It is important not to undervalue yourself in your current situation and you must present an argument that demonstrates where you stand in the event you aren't able to get the job you're looking for.

3. This is not correct. To prove your worth, you should highlight your strengths that aren't being used at the moment and are going to be used when you are assigned to a new job.

Finding new work is an excellent opportunity to grow your career. If you make an appropriate time and concentrate on your achievements, and prove your worth and worth, you're likely to be viewed as someone with plans and is ready to do the work to achieve what you desire.

Question

Which strategies do you think you can employ to solicit assignments that will help you advance your career?

Options:

1. Discuss how you'll utilize your experience in sales to create additional savings for the business when you're given a larger sales area

2. If you receive a poor performance evaluation, you fix some of the mistakes before requesting a fresh assignment

3. Write about how you've improved the productivity of your department. Also, describe what you'd do to bring that same amount of effort to be responsible for preparing all the reports required by the department.

4. Make sure you know all the information about the job before you speak to your boss with regards to the job.

5. If you're meeting with your boss, explain the books you've read to make you suitable for the new job.

Answer

Choice 1: The first choice is the correct one. One way to ask for the assignment would be to prove your value by demonstrating the way you're more important in the new position than you are in your current position.

Alternative 2: The second choice is the correct one. Sometimes, it's not the best time to request an assignment, like the moment you've had a poor performance review which focused on your weaknesses.

Third Option: The third choice is the correct one. You must emphasize your accomplishments when seeking an assignment. Also, connect those accomplishments with what you're planning to accomplish with the next assignment.

Fourth option: The fourth choice is not true. If you are requesting an assignment, it is important to do so at the proper date. This means you must act immediately whenever you hear about an assignment which is in line with your plans.

Alternative 5: The choice isn't correct. The most effective method to request you for an assignment would be to concentrate on your achievements. It is important to highlight what you've accomplished - not just the books you've studied - and then connect your accomplishments to the things you're planning to accomplish in the new task.

Change of Career

It could be the right the right time to quit your current employer in case you aren't able to achieve your goals within the company after you've tried the possibilities of promotions or lateral shifts.

If you're ready to leave then you should consider some strategies to be able to quit this job with no burning bridges. It is important to begin an interview while you employed, and keep up your good work until you are done and make sure you quit on a friendly note.

If you follow these tips by following these strategies, you'll be in a an ideal position to change jobs and stay on the right track.

Is it the right time to go?

Is it the right time to go?

The company you work for is excellent You get along well with your colleagues and your boss loves you and you've earned an impressive record of achievements throughout the years. Why would you consider leaving?

Even if you are a fan of everything about your workplace It could be time to go. If you aren't able to achieve your goals while working there after you've tried every avenue of possibility, including promotions or lateral changes it's time to look for a new job.

How do you successfully change careers

If you're ready to go on your own then you should consider several strategies to be able to quit the job you're currently at without burning any bridges.

1. Find a job as long as you have an employment

2. Keep doing your best work until you are done.

3. Leave with a smile

How do you move forward successfully?

How do you successfully move forward?

The most effective strategy for switching careers is to conduct your job search while you working. It may seem unproductive, but many employers will be biased towards candidates who aren't employed. Don't look for jobs while working!

Although scheduling interviews around your working hours may be challenging, it's much easier than explaining the reason you're in a jobless state. Interviews can be scheduled during lunch or perhaps have a day off to arrange a few interviews.

It is not only important to look for a job when you are still working at a job, but you should be able to continue to put in the best job at the position until you quit. In one way, getting your next job may be a long time-consuming process and you'll need to build on your successes. Some management staff feel disappointed when you decide to depart from their company. If you allow your work to slide the manager may be more likely to confront your lack of performance. You might even be fired before you're prepared to quit.

There are some additional points to be aware of to ensure you continue to do your most effective work until you're done.

Value

Always add value to your work while you look for an opportunity to take on a new job. It is important to continue building upon your achievements and include them on your resume. The additional work you put in this week can have a huge impact on the next interview.

Be aware of opportunities that are emerging.

It is possible that you believe there are no possibilities at your current company However, you could be mistaken. If you continue to do the best you can, a new job that matches your needs might be in your future.

Take a look at your references

There are many companies that have rules against providing references, however the one you work for might not. Make sure to ask your employer about it and you'll be given a high-quality report if you continue to deliver excellent work during your job search.

In the end, when you change careers it is important to depart with a friendly attitude. This means not burning any bridges in the process of getting out. While it might be enjoyable for a moment to smack your boss, you may end up paying the price for a long time to come. It's also not professional. It is important to be positive and helpful to your boss as well as colleagues as you leave. Even if it's been a difficult time at work and are leaving in a positive manner will boost the chances of your boss to recall you in a positive way.

You can search while you are still employed. an opportunity to work

"When I was in search of a new job, conducted all my research during working hours. I posted resumes on Sunday nights and then made follow-up calls during lunchtime in the off-site. Then I set up interviews in the early morning or when I had finished my working at the end of the day. It was not simple, but I managed it."

Continue to put in your best work until you are done.

"I set a goal of making sure I met all deadlines even though I was in search of an opportunity to get a new job. I was forced to work longer hours but this did help keep my energy levels high. I was still feeling a sense of fulfillment working. The highlight was the excellent letter of recommendation that the boss gave me!"

Leave in good terms

"When I left my employer I was inclined to confront my boss with every single thing I did not like about him. But I remembered that it won't bring me anywhere. In reality, Frank, one of my colleagues, quit the company in recent times, but he recently came to work in a new position. I was definitely looking to remain flexible and to leave on good terms."

Sometimes the only way that to achieve your goals in career is to switch to a different organization.

If you conduct an employment search when you working and doing the best you can until you are done and then leaving on pleasant terms and with a positive attitude, you'll be in a great position to make a successful transition and stay on the right track.

Question

Are there examples of ways you can be successful in moving to a new employer?

Options:

1. You're still able to submit your report one day earlier even though you're in search of an opportunity to get a new job

2. You think your boss was unfair to you You decide to let it go behind your head as you begin to move on to a new job

3. It is a Wednesday vacation day and you schedule 2 interviews for the day, and two interviews in the afternoon.

4. You can bring the policies and procedures guides from your previous employer to the new job since they may contain helpful suggestions.

5. If you do contract with flu-like symptoms it's not a reason to call in sick for work in the last week of your vacation because you're worried that your boss will think that you're fake.

Answer

Choice 1: The first one is the best option. When you're trying to find an opportunity You should perform your best at the current position until you are done.

Alternative 2: The second one is the correct one. One way to make a career change successful is to leave your employer on good terms. This is to avoid burning bridges in your way to leave.

Third Option: The third choice is the correct one. One way to change jobs is to conduct a job search while you working. While it is challenging to plan interviews during your working hours it is best to schedule interviews during lunch breaks or perhaps schedule a day off and arrange for several interviews.

Fourth option: The fourth choice is not correct. It is recommended to follow the policies and procedure manuals that are issued by the new company to ensure that you're adhering to their rules and regulations.

Alternative 5: The one is not correct. It is best to use sick days only when needed. It's impossible to perform at your best when you're in work when you're sick.

Chapter 11: Managing The Performance Appraisal

The preparation for an annual performance Appraisal

The preparation is essential to the success of your annual appraisal of performance. You'll need to collect evidence of your results and achievements, then plan the speech you'll use to discuss important issues and anticipate being able to receive constructive criticism.

The importance of appraisal for performance

The importance of appraisal for performance

Your annual appraisal of your performance is quickly coming up. You're worried about what your employer might discover to criticize, and you're be concerned that no one will pay attention to your accomplishments in the last year. Will anyone even realize that you're the perfect candidate for that new job? It's entirely up to you.

The content of your performance evaluation can assist you in supporting what you do, demonstrate your professional growth, and demonstrate your worth. However, your employer could utilize the documents to justify reassignment or discipline and even dismissal.

Even performance appraisals from years ago could have an impact decades later when you are applying for a promotion, you ask for a raise or when you are applying for the job of your dreams. These are reasons to make every opportunity to plan for what you'll make and say in your appraisal.

Question

How much effort is your annual appraisal of performance?

Options:

1. I am meticulously prepared

2. I do some preparation

3. I like to just wing it

Answer

1. It's good to be prepared for your appraisal of performance But don't be tempted to base your decisions on too much speculation. When you receive your appraisals take a look at the criteria you'll be judged on and be ready to explain the way you performed in achieving the performance objectives.

2. It's a good idea to prepare but you must prepare thoroughly for a performance evaluation. You must be able to demonstrate your achievements and deal constructively when critics are coming at you.

Option 3. If you don't plan your appraisal for performance, then you're missing an opportunity worth taking advantage of. Keep in mind that performance appraisals are essential for making sure your career is on the right path.

The performance appraisal process is an important opportunity to control your career. In many cases, it's the one period of the year in which you receive your employer's total and unwavering attention. It's crucial to make use of the time you have to be evaluated wisely. It's not the time to be gathering with friends or discussion of ideas for improvements to the system at work. It's all about your career and you. Performance appraisals offer a variety opportunities.

Performance

Assessing yourself against the performance standards of your appraisal will help you comprehend your responsibility. The objective and fair standards serve as an objective basis to assess and evaluate your performance. They also aid in creating an understanding, which is clear and shared of the expectations for performance.

Planning

In a performance appraisal you find out if you're meeting the expectations. You evaluate your employer's expectations and the extent to which you're meeting them. This gives you the chance to devise the plan of action to creating goals and making changes.

Potential

Promotions are typically based on the performance of employees. Performance appraisals are your opportunity to state what you'd like from your work and where you'd like to be in the near future. If you talk to the company you work for, you could also inquire about opportunities for training and development.

Certain employees prefer to treat appraisals for their performance like a dental exam an unpleasant meeting in which the tangible evidence of negligence is revealed to them. Some may view appraisals to criticize or complain or even to vent their frustrations with colleagues. However, what they fail to realize is that appraisals for performance is about improving and not blaming.

Most importantly, it's crucial to your career performance evaluation be an enjoyable satisfaction for you as well as your employer. An effective review clears cloud of the past and establishes the stage for a successful future.

Question

What opportunities do your annual performance evaluation offer?

Options:

1. It is a platform for setting your goals and describing your achievements

2. You can determine if you're meeting the expectations of your employer

3. You can gain a better understanding of your job responsibilities by evaluating yourself against the performance standards.

4. This is a great opportunity to talk about issues you've experienced with colleagues

5. It's the perfect moment to suggest general improvements to the workplace system.

Answer

Choice 1: It's the good choice. A performance review is the best spot to discuss your goals for the future and proving them by your previous accomplishments.

Option 2. This is a right choice. It's impossible to meet your the expectations of your clients if you're unclear about what they are. It is not advisable to make preconceived notions.

Option 3. This is the good choice. The criteria your company uses to assess performance can be useful indicators to determine the priorities of your work.

Option 4 The wrong choice. Your performance appraisal isn't a moment to discuss colleagues. Performance appraisals are about improving not blaming.

Option 5 Option 5: This is a bad choice. The performance appraisal you receive is not an appropriate time to make general comments about your work environment. Any suggestions must be specific to your work and you.

Making preparations for a performance evaluation

Making preparations for a performance evaluation

It's a sad fact that many employees attend their appraisals for performance with little or no preparation. Remember that there's no benefit to not having a plan. It's not fun being surprised by a situation you didn't expect or fail to make the most of an opportunity during your evaluation.

Unprepared to defend your position or advance your career goals , you'll end up in an active or passive role instead of a productive one. Making sure you are prepared to give your appraisal will allow you to concentrate on the main issue - improving your performance.

There are a variety of activities that will assist you in preparing your performance appraisal

* obtaining evidence of your accomplishments and performance,

* planning what you'll say on the most important issues, and

* eager to receive constructive critique.

Gathering evidence

Prior to your appraisal, collect evidence of your results and achievements so you can back up your position in a positive way - the first activity to prepare. Remember that the annual performance appraisal is a metric of your performance throughout the course of the year. However, all human judgements are subjective to a certain degree.

When you gather evidence of positive results and achievements that you can back the positive view or even contest a negative judgement. Be sure that your evidence is precise, up-to current, and in line with standard of excellence.

The evidence provides objective data about your accomplishments in meeting the demands in your work. For instance, do you work selling? If you've hit your sales goals, do you have the data and facts available to support your claims.

It's also crucial to save copies of your previous evaluations. This will let you demonstrate the success you have achieved in achieving your goals as well as enhancing your standard of performance.

Ramesh has been appointed the Assistant Manager of Ramesh is the assistant manager of the Admitting Department at a large urban hospital. He is hoping for a promotion to manager in about two years. Keep reading as he discusses the methods he uses to gather proof of his performance and achievements to present during his appraisal of performance.

Because I am in contact with the public, one my standards of performance includes "Communicate with a variety of people about a range of subjects."

The documentation I provide in my performance evaluation should be able to show the kind of information I've shared and who I've communicated it to.

Over the course of this time, I've kept a list of incidents in which communication was a concern. In cases where privacy wasn't an issue, I've maintained documents, reports and e-mails that I've written in response to complaints, providing details, explanations or a response to complaints.

I also take note of the method and time I collected the evidence to prove that it's current and pertinent to the performance standards.

Question

Emelia works for a big graphic design company. Her technical review of her most recent annual appraisal revealed that she was able to improve her skills in designing software.

What are some instances of Emelia accumulating evidence of her results and achievements to be used in her annual appraisal of performance?

Options:

1. Emelia is able to gather examples of advertisements she was a part of throughout the year.

2. Emelia has copies of previous appraisals

3. Emelia emphasizes her goal of enhancing her design skills and creates a copy of the award she received in her design software class.

4. Emelia decides to demonstrate her creativity by inventing her responses to appraiser's questions

5. Emelia creates a career strategy for her employer to display at the time of appraisal.

Answer

Choice 1: It's the right choice. Emelia is aware of the need to be prepared for the evaluation by presenting her achievements.

Option 2: This is the good choice. Emelia could use her previous appraisals to prove she achieved her goals and improved her performance in relation to the standards of performance.

Third option: It is the right choice. Emelia's course certification is proof that she has achieved her goal of developing her computer skills.

Option 4 4. This is a bad choice. Emelia requires proof to back her achievements.

Option 5 It's a bad choice. While discussing career plans can be crucial, it isn't related to Emelia collecting evidence of her good results and achievements.

The preparation of what to say

Making a list of what you want to say

While you won't be able to know exactly how your annual appraisal will be conducted, it will aid in preparing your remarks on crucial issues. This is the third of three tasks.

Prior to your evaluation, you should take the time to think about the types of issues that you believe will be dealt with. Consider any questions or remarks your employer might have and consider the appropriate response.

As an example Have you encountered obstacles or challenges that affected your work performance? Prepare to talk about the way you dealt with those issues and what you'd change differently to make your performance better in the future.

You must be prepared to talk about concerns in a variety of crucial areas throughout your assessment:

* your job description,,

* achievements since your last appraisal

* The rating of the performance standards,

* Any areas that could be improved or further development

* what are your plans for the future and

*Your self-assessment.

Watch as Ramesh describes how he is preparing what he'll discuss at his next performance evaluation in the hospital.

In preparation for my assessment I was thinking about what I would like to achieve. In the end, my appointment is just an hourlong, and I decided that I'd need to prepare for the things I'll be saying.

My supervisor will retire in the next two years, and my goal is to be the head in the hospital's Admitting Department. I'll face candidates for the position and I must start the process now.

For instance, in the last year, there were various issues that occurred in the event that patient records were misplaced for a period of time and resulted in delays in admission. I'm sure this issue could be an issue when I am evaluating my administration skills So I've made sure that I'm well-aware of the circumstances, and developed some procedure changes to the system.

Naturally, I'm not able to predict the exact questions my employer will ask me however I can think about the kinds of questions that might be asked. If I plan out what I'm likely to say, I'm able to transform a negative into positive. Instead of being caught off guard by the issue, I'm going make use of it to showcase my ability to adapt and my administrative capabilities.

Question

Which are the finest examples of Emelia's preparing her remarks on key questions that could be raised during her forthcoming performance evaluation for the graphic design firm?

Options:

1. Emelia is preparing to discuss the issue that led to an important client quitting the company for another company.

2. Emelia anticipates the questions her employer could ask and designs answers for them.

3. Emelia creates a plan of action for her future with the company.

4. Emelia decides that her supervisor is going to inquire to improve her technical abilities and she begins to prepare

to discuss the course of study she's completed

5. Emelia ensures she's dressed in a professional way

6. Emelia makes sure she's made copies of all documents that she needs to be filed with her supervisor's file

Answer

1. This would be the right choice. Emelia must prepare to talk about how she handled issues and challenges, as well as what she might take to enhance her performance in the future.

2. This option is the good choice. The model answers will assist Emelia to prepare for the questions her boss may ask during her appraisal.

3. This would be the right choice. Emelia should be prepared for the possibility of relating her

career goals to her appraisal of performance and discuss her plans for the future.

4. This option is the good option. Emelia must prepare to talk about how she's achieved her goals for performance.

Option 5 The wrong alternative. It's important to dress appropriately however it's not a an element of planning the way you'll address key questions.

Option 6 It's a bad choice. Making additional copies of documents is a part the process of gathering information, but not part of preparing the way you'll address key aspects of the appraisal.

Being subject to criticism

Being subject to criticism

The feeling of being judged isn't pleasant However, it's also necessary. The most valuable aspects you can get from a performance assessment is knowing the areas in which your performance isn't in line with your employer's expectations.

Criticism is not always an unfavorable thing. In fact you should be looking forward to constructive criticism of your assessment. In a sense it's a gift. It helps you to understand the way others view your actions.

It's crucial to avoid the urge to react emotionally. When you're prepared for criticism, you'll be more likely to respond in a positive and productive ways.

Even if you expect to receive negative or unfair criticism take advantage of the chance to determine the reason you're being viewed in this way and also why your performance isn't achieving expectations.

Remember, if you're willing to accept the legitimacy of your employer's opinions and performance scores It shows that you're dedicated to learning and improving your performance at work.

A constructive critique can open numerous possibilities for you to use when you're evaluating your performance and you'll have the chance to show your commitment and receptive attitude

Employers can see they are serious in your your performance you can show your employer that you're serious about performance

You can identify opportunities to develop your abilities and skills that will help you be more appealing

Watch as Ramesh describes how he prepares for criticism during his performance evaluation in the hospital.

In the past, when I gave performance appraisals I wasn't always in agreement with my rating. In this year's performance appraisal, I'm determined keep my eyes open. I'm willing to hear the things my employer has to say even if I don't agree with his opinion, I'll exhibit an attitude of acceptance towards his critique.

In the past, I was irritated over the comments of my boss. But expressing anger wasn't effective. This year, I've prepared myself to address critiques in a calm, rational way. It shows the boss I'm determined to improve my performance.

I'm also ready to take my evaluation to gain an advantage. For instance, I'm confident that I have the potential to develop my organizational abilities. If an opportunity presents itself during my evaluation, I'm likely recommend a mentorship program with the hospital's chief administrator.

Question

Anne has been employed since 2002 as a professional support staff in an insurance firm.

Her first appraisal was a disappointment. Anne was irritated by the lack of sensitivity in her boss's assessment of her writing skills. This year Anne is determined to improve her skills to respond to his critique.

What are the most effective examples of Anne eagerly anticipating being constructively critiqued during her appraisal of performance?

Options:

1. Anne prepares emotionally to be ready to hear her boss's critique

2. Anne plans how she'll react positively to criticisms she could get in her appraisal

3. Anne is working on some ideas for training opportunities she'd like to investigate to enhance her communication skills

4. Anne has letters to show how her writing skills have improved.

5. Anne plans what she'll tell her boss if she is asked about her career aspirations for the near future.

Answer

1. This would be the appropriate choice. Staying calm and professional and listening to what her

boss says will assist Anne show that she has an open and responsive mindset.

Option 2. This is a good option. Being prepared to address the criticisms will assist Anne convince her boss that she's committed to improving performance.

3. This could be the good choice. It is crucial for Anne to take positive action when faced with criticism and to be prepared to seize opportunities to develop her abilities.

Option 4 4. This is a bad alternative. The gathering of evidence to prove your accomplishments is crucial however it's not a part of the process of preparing yourself mentally to take constructive criticism.

Option 5 It's a bad alternative. The preparation of what to talk about your career goals can be helpful however it's not an aspect of looking forward to constructive criticism.

How to Make the Most of Your Annual Performance Evaluation

The most important aspect of your performance evaluation will be a review on your achievements. It is the time to present your achievements. Be confident and clear Be concise, stay on the topic and recognize the contribution of other people.

Your appraisal session is an opportunity to seek feedback that is constructive. Recognize the value of the feedback. Ensure you remain calm and unrepentant Ask for clarification of the comments that are unclear, and then discuss with your employer how to create an improvement plan.

Recognizing strategies

Recognizing strategies

The day for your annual performance appraisal is coming up. You've completed the first step of preparation. It involved collecting evidence of your achievements and preparing what you'll say about the most important topics, and preparing your emotionally to face critique. After you've established that foundation, it's moment to begin thinking about the next stage , which is presentation. This is about how to present yourself at the appraisal meeting.

Performance appraisals are crucial for your professional development, which is why you'll have to pay attention to ways of achieving control and clarity during the actual procedure.

While your employer is the one in charge of this meeting, it's involved in the process of conducting an effective appraisal.

There are two major goals in your performance appraisal meeting.

* Present your achievements and

* Seek specific corrective actions.

Presenting accomplishments

Presenting accomplishments

The most important goal is to showcase your achievements to your employer.

If you were preparing for the performance review, it is important to have collected evidence of the major achievements you would like to highlight at the meeting.

The next step is how to present this information in the most effective way. Consider the way you'll be perceived by others in presenting your achievements to your employer in the time of your evaluation.

Be confident and clear

Your words should be clear and confidently. Make sure not to sound arrogant , or "full about yourself." Do not appear cocky and frightened, or even defensive. Utilize numbers and dates to explain how your achievements correspond to your professional goals.

Stay on the topic

You're going to be given a only a short amount of time therefore it's important to be on the right track when the presentation of your achievements. Don't spend time rehashing old grievancesor talking about irrelevant or unnecessary issues. Give the information you wish to be to be known about your career goals such as. Be focused, and should your employer diverge from the the topic, gently bring it back to the original point.

Recognize the other

Have you ever seen an award program on television? It's not often that winners give their thanks to their colleagues and employers. They understand that it's essential to build a successful career by giving the credit to those who deserve it. Recognition of others is a sign that the team spirit, and will show your leadership capabilities.

Mika is currently undergoing an evaluation of her performance at the firm where she works as an assistant manager. Check out Mika's individual statements for a detailed analysis of how she explains her accomplishments.

Mika The letters we received from our clients reveal how happy they were in the rebranding effort. I thoroughly enjoyed my role as team leader and am looking to repeat the project.

Narrator: Mika is clear and confident when she gives the evidence of her achievements to her employer and also outlines her desire to lead another project.

Mika Says: I'm happy to report that the rebranding effort was completed on time and on budget.

Narrator: Mika keeps to the fact when describing her achievements in the rebranding process. She is precise in her explanation of how she achieved her goals and doesn't overstate her achievements.

Mika Max has been a great help with design, and Lee was able to negotiate a significant price in exchange for air time. In reality, our team was extremely hard at work to ensure that the client needed to be satisfied.

Narrator says that when Mika acknowledges her teammembers, it shows that she appreciates the achievements of other people. This shows both her empathy as well as her leadership capabilities.

You've completed your performance appraisal with Antoinette. If you were confident and clear and focused on the issue and acknowledged the contributions of the other employees You can call this a satisfactory performance appraisal.

Question

You are employed by a company that is involved in renovations and construction. In the last year, you've been involved in various projects and even your first one as a project manager.

What are the most effective examples of how you can present your achievements in your annual performance appraisal?

Options:

1. "I possess the bank statement of the restaurant venture I was a part of which proves that we made it on time and within our budget."

2. "We were able to meet the client's requirements on all project I was involved in this past year."

3. "My coworker Barrett was an excellent resource working with the customers on the restaurant's development."

4. "Well I was able to help with the museum's work However, Lee was the main one to do his work."

5. "When our team worked on our university project, a fascinating incident occurred to our team at the work site."

Answer

Choice 1: It's the good choice. You're confident and clear when communicating your achievements and providing the proof of your accomplishments.

Option 2. This is the right choice. If you write down your particular achievement, you're trying that you are on the right track in describing your achievements.

Option 3. This is a good choice. In acknowledging Barrett's contribution you demonstrate that you are aware of the accomplishments of other people and also your own.

4. This one isn't correct. While it's essential to acknowledge the contributions of others, you should not deny your part in the success. In this situation you're not clear or confident in presenting your achievements.

Alternative 5: The choice is not correct. It's good to be confident however, you should not wander off the topic. This wastes time and energy.

Looking for correctional input

Looking for an appropriate input

After you've presented your achievements, the next most important step to increase the efficiency of your performance evaluation is to take specific corrective actions to enhance your performance.

The purpose of your performance appraisal is the evaluation of your past and current performance as well as finding out your potential and potential value to your company in the future.

Be aware that achieving the things your employer believes are essential is crucial to your advancement. Consider your evaluation as an ideal moment to understand your strengths and weaknesses in your job.

The process of seeking corrective action could provide you with the chance to grow professionally and can be an opportunity to resolve issues with your performance, and can help you become more effective at what you do.

What causes negative feedback in the time of a performance evaluation

Negative feedback could be the result of different reasons: misunderstandings or a mistake by you, different views on what's important, comparing yourself to colleagues, or failing to perform as per standards. Whatever the reason, the most important aspect is to utilize the criticism you receive to improve your performance.

You can employ strategies to take corrective action and use negative feedback into positive Recognize the value of feedback

Be calm and non-retaliatory

Ask for clarification of unclear remarks ask for clarification of vague comments

Work with your employer to create an improvement plan with your employer.

You might not be happy with the negative feedback, but it's essential to acknowledge an employer's valid basis for expressing that critique.

Be aware that employers are able to interpret information in the way they see it. It's in your favor to accept the truthfulness of feedback and discover ways you can enhance your performance as they see it.

Criticism can be hurtful. It's essential to stay cool and unrepentant in the event of a poor assessment. If you're willing to accept and are interested in the criticisms shows that you're open to improvements.

Employers aren't all experts in communicating. You should ensure you know what your boss will be saying when they provide feedback. If you want clarification on vague remarks it is helpful to clarify the criticism , and then ask for clarification. For instance, you could say "You observed that I wasn't great with managing my time. Why is that?"

When you've identified what you need to improve It's now time to collaborate with your employer on improvements plans. It's crucial that you can agree on the improvements which will have the biggest impact on time and energy as well as your career progression.

The improvement plan you create is a particular course of action that specifies the actions you'll take in the future, when and how your progress will be evaluated. This is the plan you'll be using during the next evaluation period to increase your performance.

Mika is currently going through her performance appraisal with the workplace where she is employed. Check out each of Mika's remarks to see how she is seeking corrections during her appraisal.

Mika: It's right to highlight the problems caused by my late deadline in the month of March. Are there any procedural adjustments to stop the same thing from repeating itself?

Narrator: Mika acknowledges the validity of her employer's concerns when she explains that she missed an important deadline. The fact that she seeks corrective feedback suggests she's interested in what her employer considers crucial.

Mika: You pointed out that Jonathan claimed that we had lost a customer and blamed it on my work. Are you able to offer any ideas on how this incident can be dealt with better in the future?

Narrator: Mika remains calm and unrepentant when confronted by the accusations of her coworker. The employee avoids being defensive by adopting a an approach to solving problems and focusing on the future.

Mika: Could you explain what you mean by I can be more effective in managing clients?

Narrator: Mika asks her boss to clarify the vague suggestion that she needs to "be more efficient" when handling clients. Specific suggestions and examples will ensure that both she and her boss have an knowledge of the concept "better" is.

Mika: I've jotted down your most important comments. I'd love it if we could integrate your suggestions in an improvement strategy for following appraisal period.

Narrator: Mika demonstrated she was willing to collaborate with her boss in order to create the plan for improvement. This shows that she is motivated to work towards constant improvements and demonstrates the dedication of both Mika as well as her employer to her professional path.

Question

You've completed the first portion of your performance appraisal at the construction firm. Your employer has completed their appraisal and have asked whether there is anything more to be done prior to concluding.

What are the most effective examples of how to use strategies to search for specific corrective input?

Options:

1. "I am aware of your concerns about the manner in which the team I worked with communicated with customers regarding the project I supervised."

2. "I don't remember having submitted any invoices late such as the ones you have mentioned. Let's talk about the submission process to ensure I follow the proper procedure to follow in the near future."

3. "You mentioned that I should be more open in meetings. Can you provide me with an instance?"

4. "I'd like to talk about the setting of goals and measures to make improvements over the next year."

5. "No. Absolutely nothing other than that. Thank you for your comments on my work performance."

6. "'I'm not thrilled to hear that somebody said I had been late in submitting invoices. It was an accounting issue and but not my fault."

Answer

1. This option is the right choice. This statement confirms the authenticity of the feedback from your employer.

Option 2: This is the right choice. This is a good illustration of staying neutral and not retaliating when confronted with criticism.

Option 3: This is the right choice. One of the most important aspects of seeking input from a professional is asking for clarification of any vague statements.

4. This option is the right choice. The corrective approach is the base for continuous improvement throughout the year. It is essential to collaborate with your employer to develop an improvement strategy.

Option 5 The incorrect choice. This is the time you need to move to the next part of your appraisal of performance. It's crucial to take advantage of this opportunity to showcase your achievements and come up with the corrective actions you want to take.

Option 6 is not a good choice. If you don't agree with the negative feedback, it is important to remain calm and unrepentant. Your employer likely wouldn't have raised this issue in the first place if it weren't deemed to be to be valid.

Utilizing the Periodic Appraisal Strategy

The method of periodic appraisal is a reliable and efficient method of turning performance reviews into a continuous process and get your career in the right direction. It comprises twelve appraisals that include an annual appraisal as well as three quarterly appraisals as well as eight appraisals per month.

The annual, quarterly and monthly reports boost your chances of promotion by frequently reviewing your achievements, pointing out the skills you require to develop, and assisting you to keep a positive rapport with the boss.

The periodic appraisal technique

The periodic appraisal technique

Your annual appraisal of performance is done. This is an immense relief. You don't need to think about it again for another year. Right?

Question

What is the most frequent time you believe a appraisal of performance should be conducted?

Options:

1. Every year, once

2. Twice per year

3. Each month

Answer

Option 1: Take a moment to think about it for a second. Are you really willing to be waiting another year to see how you're doing?

Option 2: Fair. You could still miss out on opportunities to build your career.

Option 3: Great. While you shouldn't be spending more time evaluating rather than doing the task, the more often you review your performance the greater chance you'll have the ability to benefit from opportunities to improve and correct your behaviors. Every month, you can get a good balance.

It's possible to have an official appraisal once per calendar year but, in the real you're constantly receiving feedback about your performance. If your customers are satisfied or not, they're measuring your ability. If your colleagues are supportive or fail to support you They're sending you an email. If your bosses appreciate or dismiss you They're telling how important you are to them. This feedback can be used to improve your performance continuously.

The annual appraisal of your performance is only one element of an appraisal system.

In reality, appraisal of performance is most efficient when it's part of an ongoing exchange of performance associated information that you share with your employers.

Performance appraisals were traditionally an annual event where employees were told about areas in which their performance was not up to par and what their goals to improve their performance were. However, modern companies are encouraging the idea of periodic performance appraisals which is a process that allows both employees and employers to improve their performance continuously.

You've heard of the phrase "Out of sight and out of mind." The regular performance appraisal method helps you keep your performance as well as your goals for your career in the eye. It raises awareness of your performance, accomplishments and your protability regularly. A regular contact with your employer will help you spot and rectify performance issues when they arise, prior to your career is negatively affected.

The employer usually arranges and supervises your annual appraisal of your performance and it's your employer's responsibility to plan and conduct it.

However, the implementation of an annual appraisal plan is the initiative of the employee. It's important to let employers know about what you're going to do and get their help.

Rememberthat this strategy is about improving performance. Your boss will be more enthused to your plan by knowing how your support is tied to your company's goals.

Implementing periodic appraisals

Implementing periodic appraisals

Typically the periodic appraisal process is a monthly cycle which includes your annual appraisal as well as three quarterly appraisals along with eight quarterly appraisals. It's twelve monthly parts which are crucial for capturing your contributions to the business, and how far you've come towards your objectives.

Twelve crucial documents are created in a routine appraisal process.

Annual appraisal

The annual appraisal is held every year. It's a formal gathering where your performance in the workplace is assessed and measured, and your future goals are set. Your performance in the past year is analyzed and rated in accordance with predetermined standards for performance.

Quarterly appraisal

The quarterly appraisals are held three times per year. These are informal occasions to talk to your employer in a face-to face meeting to determine how far you've come towards your goals, and what adjustments are needed to be implemented.

Monthly appraisal

The monthly interim reviews are self-evaluations that are written and are held during the last eight months of the year.

The month of February was when Mika completed her year-end appraisal of performance at the company in which she is employed. Watch as Mika talks about how she makes use of regular performance appraisals to ensure continuous improvement.

At the time of my annual appraisal of performance my supervisor pointed out that two areas of improvement included my time management skills as well as my capacity to effectively communicate the needs of customers with my colleagues.

My method of increasing my performance and proving that I'm deserving of promotions is to make appraisals of performance an continuous process. Every month, I take the first step towards my annual appraisal.

Question

What is the difference between an annual performance review and distinct from quarterly and monthly reviews?

Options:

1. In an annual appraisal, work performance is assessed by your employer based on the pre-determined guidelines

2. A performance appraisal every year is the only chance to boost your career

3. Annual appraisals are scheduled and mandated by your employer.

4. An annual appraisal is an informal sessions of appraisal

Answer

Choice 1: The first choice is the correct one. In the time of your annual review, you performance is assessed informally. The quarterly reviews are informal gatherings and monthly reviews are self-assessments.

2. This choice is not correct. The monthly and quarterly appraisals are essential to boost your performance as well as build an argument for your promotion.

Third Option: The third choice is the correct one. The process of initiating and implementing annual appraisals of employees is the responsibility of employers.

The 4th selection is not correct. Annual appraisals are formal, documented appraisals of performance made by employers.

Your boss will not be able to see, hear or feel anything you perform at work. Your quarterly appraisals provide informal ways to provide evidence of your accomplishments and your potential for advancement. It is important to record these meetings by providing a factual assessment of your performance over the last three months. Make a single-page overview of the meeting including copies to your boss and the appraisal file.

The quarterly review can provide numerous advantages. If you inform your boss of your appraisals, it will show dedication, excellent communication abilities, and the desire to work on improving.

If you present your boss with innovative ideas, you show enthusiasm, professionalism and skill.

Finally If you are able to detect problems early and develop solutions for the issues your boss will view you as an asset.

When you meet with your quarterly bosses or your employer, it is important to talk about what you've accomplished during the quarter as well as the things you'll need to do to be successful in the near future. There are many topics you can discuss:

* exceptional achievements

* Your goals and the steps you've taken to reach them

* any other recognition or award received by your customers, clients or coworkers.

* any training you've completed or are planning to learn more about,

* your goals for your career,

* problems you anticipate arising soon and

* projects or initiatives you'd like to take on.

Follow the conversation as Mika talks about how she utilizes quarterly appraisals of performance as part of a regular appraisal process.

My quarterly appraisals occur every year three times The first appraisal is three months following my appraisal for the year. This is the time to meet with my boss and inform him of what I'm doing.

Also, I make sure that I receive feedback from my boss on my performance, specifically towards increasing my time management and communication abilities. I truly believe that this feedback can help us bond.

Following my meeting make an overview of what was discussed and then share it with my boss.

Question

What distinguishes quarterly appraisals from monthly or annual appraisals?

Options:

1. The quarterly appraisals help you spot and fix problems with performance when they occur.

2. The quarterly appraisal is an informal opportunity to talk with your employer

3. A quarterly appraisal doesn't require you to meet with your employer.

4. Quartly appraisals are formal appraisals of your performance, arranged by your employer

Answer

1. This choice is the correct one. The quarterly appraisals provide an opportunity to check in with your employer to confirm that you're heading in the right direction.

Alternative 2: The second one is true. The quarterly appraisals are informal gatherings. The annual appraisals have formal events and monthly appraisals do not require any meetings.

3. This selection is not correct. The monthly appraisals are self-assessments. These appraisals can be informal occasions to have a face-to-face meeting and discuss your work with the employer.

4. This choice is not correct. The annual appraisal of performance is the responsibility of the employer, however, completing the quarterly appraisal is an employee-led initiative.

Your monthly appraisal is an essential part of your routine appraisal strategy. Monthly appraisals are self-appraisals that you write and don't require a meeting with your employer.

Question

Denys is employed by a major financial services firm. He'd like to work as a senior consultant in investment in the near future. When he was evaluating his performance every year, Denys was told he had excellent communication skills however, he must focus on areas of technical expertise like asset management.

What are the most successful examples of Denys applying the periodic appraisal method in a proper manner?

Options:

1. Denys creates an annual report that outlines his accomplishments over the past three months. He sits down with his boss to go over the report and discuss other concerns.

2. Denys makes a self-evaluation every month of his progress towards his goals. He describes the course of training that he's enrolled in, how it has aiding his asset management abilities and how his track record has been improved.

3. Denys keeps a notepad whenever the progress he has made towards his goals. He then compiles his notes into a single assessment report at the close of the year.

4. Denys creates a report every year, but is in contact with his boss every quarter to discuss his career plans and workplace issues.

5. Denys has meetings with his supervisor every month to assess his performance.

Answer

1. This choice is the correct one. Denys should check in with his supervisor each quarter following his annual review to determine how he's doing and what adjustments he must make.

Alternative 2: The second one is the best option. In his regular appraisal method, Denys needs to write an appraisal mini each month detailing his goals as well as the related activities, measures of success, and the results.

Third Option: The third choice is not the right one. To ensure that his regular appraisal strategy continues to be successful, Denys needs to do an appraisal of some kind every month.

4. This choice is not true. The periodic appraisal technique includes quarterly, monthly, quarterly, and monthly reports.

Alternative 5: The choice is not correct. Denys must prepare a report every month, however Denys only has to sit down with his supervisor once a quarter.

Conclusion

It's your turn now to decide if you want to be in control of your life, or want to be subdued by it. Are you prepared to break the mold of the average? Are you ready to lead something more than average? Do you want to live the type of lifestyle that people imagine? If your answer is yes, then your on the correct road. Let's look at the things you have to do to live a better life than the average.

In the first place, you must to realize that you are able to make a positive transformation to your lifestyle. There is no need to rely on the help of others or the power of a single miracle to change the tide of your life. Start by making small and subtle adjustments to your routine. In time you'll be able to implement larger and more significant changes to your routine. With persistence, you will eventually get you to the point of your life where you'll be able to fully escape from the dreadful stagnation you're in. However, remember that change starts by you. Socrates stated, "The secret of change is to concentrate all of your efforts, not on fighting against the old, but rather on creating an entirely new."

The next step is to break out of your comfortable zone. The majority of people find this step the most difficult. They are so comfortable within their comfort zones that even the slightest indication of fear or a the lack of stability in their daily lives could make them scream in a panic. If you want to get ahead of the pack it is necessary to get out of your familiar zone. You must be ready to take a step back from the things that make you feel secure. You must be prepared to risk it all. As Osho has said many times, "Death is secure, life is uncertainty. Someone who really would like to live must live in in perpetual danger. Anyone who would like to climb the tops must take the chance of falling off. If you want to reach the highest peaks must be prepared for the possibility of falling off from somewhere and falling down." This means that you could be thrown down a few times when you're first moving outside of your comfort zone However, you need to simply keep going forward, without doubts or fears.

Third step the crucial one. This is the moment in your life at which you realize that there is enough and you wish to live an improved and more fulfilling life. This is when you begin making important decision. These include eliminating people from your life who have negatively influencing you, starting to take care of your body and mind well by giving your body with the right nutrition it needs, working out and going on a trip to unwind and discover your passion for your preferred activities, and enjoying your the good things in your life. The most important thing you have to do to change your life is to make a solid decision to take the necessary steps. If you're going to bounce between the two sides of this choice, you'll remain in the same spot you are. To have a better life than just average, then you must conquer your thoughts and take a decisive step. Like Patricia Fripp once said, "The day you realize that you're the one in control over your own life will be the moment that you change your life."

The fourth step is to discover the purpose of your life. There's no zombie in you, your an individual. You're here to make a difference, you're here with a reason. If you're looking to lead an existence that is more than the norm, finding your purpose is crucial. Consider what that you truly enjoy doing and what is it that make you so engaged that you forget about the time, space, and you and you shift your attention to these things. When you've got these answers, you need to consider how you can use the wonderful talents you possess be of benefit to the humanity, what can you do to make a an impact, and how can you be a part of making the world better. According to Mark Twain once said, "The two most important days of your life are your birth day and when that you discover why." Get out there and figure out the purpose of your life. The feeling of emptyness or that sensation that something is missing , will disappear once you discover your reason for existence and begin living a life that is better than the normal.

The fifth step is to indulge into the lifestyles that people who are successful and wealthy take pleasure in. It is essential to begin reading regularly. Study self-improvement books, study books on psychology, and explore anything that could impact your life in a positive manner. A daily list of tasks and adhering to it is an habit that successful people adhere to. Also setting daily goals for yourself, and be sure that you meet these goals, this can help you progress quickly. Exercise is another essential part of your routine. Training keeps your body physically and mentally healthy. If you want to be able to enjoy your life and be successful then you must be physically capable of doing this. The early morning wake-up call and focusing on crucial choices, and spending time moments with your partner are all routines that people who lead beyond average lives live. So if you'd like to live a lifestyle that is exceptional, take pleasure in the lifestyles of the most successful.

This sixth stage is keeping your motivation high. There will times when you feel you're not able to continue and you're feeling depressed and confused. In these kinds of days, you'll need drive to keep going and moving ahead. Motivation can come from a variety of sources. You can read motivational tales and books, or watch motivational videos and listen motivational music and speeches. Another aspect you have to be aware of to keep yourself focused is the need to believe in yourself. You must be a believer in your cause and be convinced that the best things will be going to happen and you must be confident in your own abilities. Motivation can also be found when you give yourself a reward. If you accomplish an objective even if it's only one scoop of ice cream you should celebrate. It will help keep you motivated to continue moving forward. One wise man stated, "When you feel like giving up, think about the reason you began."

Step seven is about taking risks. You can take a chance to be in love again, no matter how deeply your heart has been broken. Be prepared to fail in the event that you take on something completely different. Remember that failure is merely an opportunity to get to the next level. Be honest with yourself. There is no need to put on an identity card in front of others. Be yourself be authentic and don't make yourself appear. If others don't like your real shades, that's their issue, not yours. Be willing to take the full accountability in your personal happiness. Your happiness isn't dependent on your situation or the people around you. Your happiness is dependent on you. If you're ever scared to take the risk keep in mind that in the end , the only thing you'll regret is the risk you chose not to choose to take.

In the end, life isn't that long. It's not immortal, and everyone's result, at the end is exactly identical. What's the reason you would wish to waste the amazing chance to live by living life in a way that is average? It's time to rise and enjoy the aroma of coffee. Do things you truly enjoy, and feel content, achieve success and become wealthy. It's okay to be unsure and it's fine to not be able to know everything, and it's fine to be a risk-taker.

www.ingramcontent.com/pod-product-compliance
Lightning Source LLC
Chambersburg PA
CBHW050401120526
44590CB00015B/1775